Testimonia

The Solution is a must read for anyone suffering with any kind of stress, anxiety, or depression. Jeremy's words are truth, vital, and so important for the world to hear. You will find the tools to completely transform your life in this book.

Dr. George Grant
Pharmaceutical Toxicologist

Jeremy gives hope to all those suffering.

Dr. Effie Chow
World renowned energy healer

Jeremy's work is transformational.

Marie Diamond
Star of, The Secret

The Solution

by Jeremy Bennett

Motivational Press
LEADERS IN GLOBAL PUBLISHING

Published by Motivational Press, Inc.
7777 N Wickham Rd, # 12-247
Melbourne, FL 32940
www.MotivationalPress.com

Copyright 2014 © by Jeremy Bennett

All Rights Reserved

No part of this book may be reproduced or transmitted in any form by any means: graphic, electronic, or mechanical, including photocopying, recording, taping or by any information storage or retrieval system without permission, in writing, from the authors, except for the inclusion of brief quotations in a review, article, book, or academic paper. The authors and publisher of this book and the associated materials have used their best efforts in preparing this material. The authors and publisher make no representations or warranties with respect to accuracy, applicability, fitness or completeness of the contents of this material. They disclaim any warranties expressed or implied, merchantability, or fitness for any particular purpose. The authors and publisher shall in no event be held liable for any loss or other damages, including but not limited to special, incidental, consequential, or other damages. If you have any questions or concerns, the advice of a competent professional should be sought.

Manufactured in the United States of America.

ISBN: 978-1-62865-109-6

Contents

Testimonials 1
Disclaimer 8
Foreword 9
Introduction 11

Chapter 1 **Forget what you've learned and open your mind.** **15**
Chapter 2 **What brought me here?** **19**
Chapter 3 **Let's start to question what we know about anxiety.** **30**
Chapter 4 **You cannot heal by pointing fingers.** **36**
Chapter 5 **Addressing the cause.** **41**
Chapter 6 **When we were babies.** **46**
Chapter 7 **The Powerhouse to your everything.** **51**
Chapter 8 **The most important part of this book!**
 It doesn't know the difference! **55**
Chapter 9 **Top things that contribute to stress and anxiety.** **57**
Chapter 10 **Top things to do to reduce stress and anxiety.** **114**
Chapter 11 **How to be grounded.** **166**
Chapter 12 **Quick fixes are not meant to be: the resilience factor.** **169**
Chapter 13 **Why do we attract what we attract?** **175**
Chapter 14 **Resting the mind.** **179**
Chapter 15 **A deeper look at meditation.** **182**
Chapter 16 **How to meditate.** **186**
Chapter 17 **The law of giving.** **190**
Chapter 18 **Why do we crave?** **193**
Chapter 19 **We all have a little darkness in us** **196**
Chapter 20 **Does everything happen for a reason?** **202**
Chapter 21 **Imagine not being from this earth.** **204**
Chapter 22 **It's the year 3000.** **210**
Chapter 23 **What does it mean to be awakened?** **213**
Chapter 24 **Going against the grain.** **215**

Other books by the author 222
Jeremy Bennett Bio 223

For Fred.

We love you.
We miss you.

Disclaimer

The content in, The Solution is generalized and presented for information and educational purposes only. No content in this book is intended to be a substitute for professional medical advice, diagnosis or treatment. You are advised to consult a qualified medical or mental health professional or any other appropriate professional regarding the applicability, opinion or recommendations with respect to your symptoms or medical conditions.

If you are experiencing any kind of medical emergency, call your doctor or the emergency services in your country immediately.

Foreword

We live in a world where stress, anxiety, and depression is growing epidemically. More kids are being "diagnosed" with ADD, ADHD, behavioural disorders, general anxiety disorders, Obsessive Compulsive Disorder, and even depression. Some people have gone so far as to call anxiety the "disease" of the 21st Century.

Being a Doctor, Nutritionist, and Pharmaceutical Toxicologist I have seem with my own eyes the debilitating effects of stress and anxiety on my patients. Year after year I seem to see younger and younger people developing a life full of crippling anxiety. What is even more unfortunate is the multitude of misinformation available to the public. We live in a society that believes that pharmaceutical drugs should be the first form of treatment when in reality it should be one of the last. Our minds and bodies are amazing, intelligent, and have the ability to heal themselves when we treat them the way we are meant to treat them.

In, The Solution Jeremy not only shows us the real cause of stress and anxiety but he does it in a way that people can relate to. I have witnessed Jeremy's live presentation on many occasions and I see first-hand the impact that he has on people all over the world.

His message is real. His message is truth. He tells it exactly the way it is supposed to be told; no beating around the bush and with concrete science. If you are suffering with stress, anxiety, or depression or know someone that is this book is an absolute must read. Even if you are not suffering with any form of mental discomfort this book will still be extremely beneficial on your journey in rewiring the brain to help you achieve the life of your dreams.

Read this book to discover the tools to reduce stress, anxiety, and depression. Read this book to learn the techniques to lives a calm, peaceful, and blissful life. But most importantly, read this book to discover how astonishingly powerful you are when you use your brain and thoughts the way that you are meant to use it. By using the techniques talked about in this book, you can and will completely transform your life.

Dr. George Grant
Pharmaceutical Toxicologist
Former Senior Consultant for Health Canada, FDA, and CDC
www.academyofwellness.com
www.your101ways.com

Introduction

My journey in the field of self-improvement started when I was a child. I have always had an interest in what the human mind was capable of. I often heard the story of an elderly woman lifting up a car to save a child trapped underneath. Where did this ability come from? Where did she acquire the strength? How can one person have the ability to tell when someone is lying? How can one person have absolutely no ability to be good in math, while it comes naturally to another person?

From the tender age of five years old, I became intrigued with the supernatural and the astonishing power of the human mind. I was always interested in stories about ghosts, hauntings, spirits, aliens, and UFOs. And I wondered what happens when we die. Ever since I could remember, I've had a burning urge to experience something that I could not explain. I've wished for this; I've prayed for this. And year after year I found myself continuing to search.

Around the same age, I became intrigued with the art of magic. I loved to fool people into thinking something was happening; when in fact, it wasn't. I loved the expression on people's faces when they witnessed the impossible. In my mind, of course, I knew they were not witnessing the impossible. Their mind was tricking them into seeing something that actually was not happening.

But that is why I was interested in this field. How could the mind trick you into seeing something that was not actually happening? This intrigued me and led me into studying the art more and more.

Most kids have an interest in magic while growing up, but eventually, it fades and a new hobby takes over. For me the hobby grew and grew. Every year I became more intrigued with the art and I found myself becoming fairly good at some more advanced card tricks and sleight of hand.

As the years went by, magic and the supernatural became my main interests. I spent a large majority of my time studying both subjects. At the age of about eighteen, I started performing magic at local schools, festivals, etc. My father drove me from place to place and helped with anything I needed. By the age of about twenty-two, I started performing professionally and formed a fairly successful business out of it. Specializing in the mind, I played with the audience's minds and performed feats of mentalism (mind magic). Performing was my favorite thing to do in life. I loved the expression on people's faces when they witnessed the "magic." They became "kid-like" again and for brief moments, while experiencing the magic, their worries seem to wither away.

This also intrigued me. How can the magic seem to put people in a better mood? How can someone who is totally stressed out go to one of my magic shows and feel calm, happy, and filled with joy? How can experiencing something seem to put someone in a better mood? Or was this all an illusion? All I knew at the time was that when they experienced the magic they felt better. This really caught my attention as it seemed as though the magic was healing them in some small way.

But what really inspired me to write this book was a journey that I went through from age twelve to about eighteen. These years of my life are fully explained in my first book, *The Power of the Mind: How I Beat OCD.*

From age twelve to about eighteen, I suffered from a very severe case of Obsessive Compulsive Disorder and depression. In the worst of these years, I was performing up to four to six hours a day of rituals (compulsions). I was not very functional and I gave up everything that I loved in life. I lost almost forty pounds in weeks. And I went from being on the top of my class to sinking to the low forties, putting myself in a position of barely passing grades seven through twelve.

I was told there was no cure for OCD and that I would always be on anti-depressants my entire life. This was devastating. As months went by, I decided not to pay attention to what I was told and to start exploring different approaches of beating what I was told I could not.

The solutions that you are about to read are the things that I have discovered throughout the years. These things changed me from a person who didn't want to get out of bed in the morning to a person that absolutely loves life. These solutions brought me from a person that was crippled with a mental disorder to a person that spends his life traveling the world educating others on the astonishing power of their minds, and loving and adoring every single second of it. These solutions opened me up to a world that replaced stress, agony, and turmoil with peace, happiness, and bliss.

No matter what your struggle is, these solutions will apply to you.

Enjoy.

Chapter 1

Forget what you've learned and open your mind.

We are brought up in a society that loves to push beliefs on us. Through marketing, journalism, and word of mouth, we are bombarded with stuff to believe. Some of these beliefs are grounded in science and truth. And some are disturbingly manipulated and ultimately have a huge detrimental effect on our health.

Growing up I was brainwashed into believing certain "truths." I took these "truths" for granted and didn't challenge them. I believed they were true because everyone else believed they were true. Our doctors, parents, teachers, and everyone else I trusted believed they were true. After all, these were people that had achieved degrees and had education to back up their claims. So why would I not believe what I was told?

It was challenging these beliefs and simply looking into other areas of "truths" that healed me. It was opening my eyes and questioning all these beliefs that I was raised into believing. It was going outside the norm and realizing that there must be something wrong with my understanding of health, life, and everything else in-between. How could the same psychologist that is telling people how to overcome depression be on antidepressants herself? Or how can a doctor's first choice of advice to eliminate illness be a drug that inevitably destroys the immune system?

There was something missing, and over the last ten+ years, I've come to understand a completely different "truth."

The human mind is absolutely astonishing at what it does. The average human body has about 60-100 trillion cells. Your cells are doing trillions and trillions of things every single second. And every single cell knows exactly what every other cell is doing the second it does it. With all of the intelligence that we know our minds have, how can we live in a society where the solution to illness is a poisonous substance created in a laboratory and mass marketed as a cure? How can we live in a society that for the most part relies on drugs to "*cure,*" and overlooks the absolutely astonishing power of the human body to heal itself if treated the way it's supposed to be treated?

We need to learn to open our minds, forget what the media is telling us, and look at the facts of health and wellbeing. We need to stop relying solely upon what we are being told and look within us for answers that we *do* have. We need to learn to question our beliefs and more importantly understand why we are taught what we are taught.

Some questions this book will explore:

What truly causes anxiety?

CHAPTER 1   **Forget what you've learned and open your mind.**

What are the misunderstandings of anxiety?

What do we do every day that contributes to anxiety?

How do we effectively reduce stress and anxiety?

Can the mind heal disease?

Can the mind create disease?

What is the explanation behind the placebo effect?

What is the nocebo effect?

What does a vengeful mind do to our health?

Can judging another person actually decrease our immune system?

What happens to the brain when we gossip?

Are the pharmaceutical companies really there to help us heal?

Are there real approaches to medicine other than western medicine?

Do we truly control our minds or do our minds control us?

What is the "ego" and where does it come from?

Why do we attract the things into our lives that we attract?

Why do some people love particular situations while the same situation triggers anxiety in another?

What happens to our health when we blame others for their behavior?

Do we have free will or is this just an illusion?

How do we get to a place where we don't take things personally anymore?

Do we control our health?

These "truths" will be revealed and discussed in this book.

I hope this book inspires you as much as it inspired me by writing it.

Chapter 2

What brought me here?

As I mentioned in the introduction, I wrote a book that was published in 2010. The book is called, *The Power of the Mind: How I Beat OCD*. This book has gone on to help tens of thousands of people all over the world in their struggle with not only OCD, anxiety, stress, or depression, but with any struggle they were/are facing. In *The Power of the Mind: How I Beat OCD*, I give the reader a deeper look at what anxiety is and challenge what we tend to think about it.

But more than anything, my previous book is a description of what I like to call my previous life of living with a crippling anxiety and depression. For many years, I suffered with a very severe case of Obsessive Compulsive Disorder and did not know what I was going through. This was a time when the Internet was just being introduced into our society, but not readily available like it is nowadays. So the multitude of information in the form of articles, blogs, videos, and social media did not exist. In other words, the symptoms I experienced were not a "click" away as they are nowadays.

Jeremy Bennett

I suffered for many years with a crippling form of OCD, which eventually led into clinical depression. My rituals grew and so did the stress and anxiety that came along with it. Without going into detail, as this book is about solutions, I will try to describe a little of what my life was like back then.

I can remember in grade seven, coming home from school, and playing ball hockey with my friends out on the street. My life revolved around playing sports every day as a kid. I loved the outdoors. Ball hockey and softball were two of my favorites. I grew up in a beautiful, small community of only about 300-400 people called Flat Bay in Newfoundland, Canada. We didn't have much to do in this place other than play ball hockey, softball, and the odd game of soccer.

I was such a happy kid, always smiling, laughing, and being goofy. There wasn't much that could bring me down back then. I was outgoing, loved to be outside, and loved to be silly. Although I was shy in certain situations, I was also goofy in the presence of people that I knew well. I had never suffered with anxiety and most certainly was not experiencing any sort of depression. I loved life as a kid.

But then life started to change at about age twelve. During the first weeks of the disorder affecting me, it wasn't serious. I was more curious than scared about what was happening, actually.

I can remember coming home one night after playing ball hockey for several hours. I went to bed and noticed that one dresser drawer was sticking out a little bit more than the others.

CHAPTER 2   What brought me here?

I tried to get to sleep but for some weird reason it was pestering me. I had an odd feeling inside me; wanting me to stand up, walk over, and push the drawer back in. I fought this for a while and thought the feeling would go away. But it didn't. I stood up, walked over, and pushed the drawer back in, and like magic, that odd feeling went away. I fell fast asleep and forgot about it.

The next night I noticed that once again, one of my dresser drawers was sticking out a little bit more than some others. That same feeling of psychological nagging revisited. I didn't know where it was coming from. It was more interesting than stressful. Once again, it was pestering enough to influence me to get out of bed, walk over, and push it in. Upon doing that the odd feeling disappeared.

As the days went on, I found life becoming a little weirder each day. I noticed that things in my possession had to be at a particular angle. If it were not, I'd experience the same feeling as when looking at the dresser drawer. So I would put everything around me at a particular angle until my mind felt right, until my body felt right. I noticed that if I walked over lines on the floor in school with my right foot first, I would experience that same nagging feeling until I retraced my steps and walked with my left foot first. As days went on I felt an urge to, when opening or closing a door, twist the knob of the door to the point where I felt it couldn't turn anymore. Then I twisted it back to the left and then to the right, over and over again. I felt the urge to tap on the lock at my locker several times with two particular fingers, and I had no idea where the urge was coming from.

All the students, friends, and teachers saw what I was doing. Many questioned why I did what I did. My response was to awkwardly laugh and walk away. I didn't know why I was doing those things, so how could I have possibly responded with any reasonable or rational answer?

As months went by, I noticed these "rituals" were increasing and the urge to do each one was becoming more severe. I didn't care who was around; I didn't care what situation I was in. When I needed to tap, walk back and forth over lines, rearrange everything around me, or repeat sentences under my breath, I was going to do it. This lead to many questions from concerned friends and family. Once again, my response to their never-ending questions was an awkward grin and to walk away.

About three years into fighting this illness, which I did not know was an illness, I became clinically depressed. Although, many people saw the switch in personality; many people didn't, as I put on a show in front of most. But when it came time to be alone, I battled my thoughts, sadness, and constant despair. I gave up practically everything I loved in life, because battling my own unwanted thoughts was draining every last bit of energy within me. Many nights I silently cried myself to sleep.

Growing up (before OCD hit me), I was always on top of my class. I graduated grade six with an average well into the nineties. But upon entering grade seven, when my symptoms of OCD started to flourish, I found studying and paying attention in class practically impossible. I quickly sank from the nineties to the forties. In grades seven through twelve, I was always in danger of failing. I knew that I had the potential to do great and my teachers knew this, but what they didn't know about was the crippling pain I suffered.

In about year two or three, the monster (as I refer to it in my first book, *The Power of the Mind: How I Beat OCD*) took on a different form. When I touched anything, or practically did anything for that matter, I would see this crystal clear image in my mind of something I didn't want to happen, happen. Usually this would be an image of a loved one dying or getting severely hurt. I would see my mother dying, my sisters getting hurt, my father in a coffin, or my brother dying while traveling. In order to go about my day, I would have to repeat what I was doing at the time of getting this image in my head, without having that image in my head. Obviously, it's extremely difficult to clear your mind of an image once it's stuck in your head. So, I found myself repeating what I was doing over and over and over again. This was becoming quite obvious to everyone in my presence. People would make fun of my actions and some would stare at me in real curiosity. I've had people think I was high on drugs, while others were as clueless as I was when performing these rituals.

I can remember eating meals and having disturbing images in my mind of something I didn't want to visualize, see, or think. And of course, I would have to repeat what I was doing, trying to do it with a clear mind, in order to get rid of that feeling. So I would chew my food, get that image in my mind, spit it out, try to chew up the same food again, get that image in my mind, spit it out again, and repeat over and over until I won and did it with a clear mind. During the year that I was suffering most, I lost about forty pounds in about four weeks.

Before/after weight loss

Years went by as this monster trapped my mind. My rituals were growing, my dark thoughts were becoming more severe, and my ability to control my compulsions was slipping away day by day.

What hurt most of all was that I didn't know what was going on. I didn't hear of Obsessive Compulsive Disorder and I was convinced that nobody on earth was going through what I was going through. I would not reach out for help because I thought I would end up in a mental institution. I didn't talk to anyone about it because I couldn't articulate into words what I was going through. To be completely honest, it's now over ten years later, and I still cannot articulate the words of what I felt back then. And if you are a sufferer, or have been a sufferer of OCD, you know exactly what I mean.

So year by year, I suffered with this crippling form of anxiety and depression. I was so lost and had no idea why I was suffering the way I was suffering. I would look around me and see my friends being happy, laughing, and enjoying life, while I suffered day after day. I didn't know why this type of suffering inflicted me. I was such a good kid. I was never in trouble at school or at home. I was nice to the people in my life and always tried my best to be as mannerly as I could. So, each day I questioned why this was happening to me. I could not understand why such a good kid could be punished with such a severe form of suffering.

My family wanted to help me every step of the way. Not only did I not accept the help, I did not know how to accept it. How could a kid accept help for something that he does not understand, on any level? How can someone decrease my urge to stop tapping or walking back and forth over lines on the floor? How could someone help me stop blinking over and over again until my mind and body felt okay?

My mind started to become what I now refer to as the master manipulator. If I heard, saw, or read anything, it would rearrange it at lightning speed into something that I dreaded to think about or visualize. This was torturous. For instance, if I walked down the street and saw a black house with black trim, my mind would go to work and instantaneously deliver up something like this: Black represents death; the trim makes up about one percent of the house. This meant that the last person I'd thought of, someone I loved, was in danger of having a child who would live one percent of a typical person's life.

How fast my mind would work to manipulate things impressed me. I have never suffered with anything like this growing up and I had no idea why my mind worked against me. We were not educated on this in school and were certainly not encouraged to speak about this in society. The stigma associated with mental illness was huge while I was growing up as a child.

So every time my mind started to manipulate things into some form of negativity, I would have to repeat what I was doing at the time that the thought entered my mind, until I could eventually do it without thinking that thought. If I could do that, then the anxiety finally went away.

Anything associated with death was particularly hard on me. My mind would have a field day with the sight of a hearse, creating all kinds of horrible images to correspond with my feelings. I'd go out of my way to avoid any things to do with death. If I caught even a glimpse of a funeral procession while I was driving, I'd turn my head and close my eyes so I couldn't see it. If a hearse passed me on the street, I'd do everything in my power not to think about somebody I cared about while it was in sight. I'd blink my eyes rapidly, pinch my leg, concentrate on my breath, or anything else that would take my mind off people that I cared about.

I constantly monitored my thoughts. Whom am I thinking about now? What am I going to see next? What are they going to say on TV? What am I going to read about in my textbook? How can I turn my head to avoid the next negative thing I see while I am in a car? It seemed like it would never end. It was physically and emotionally exhausting.

In my worst years, I was performing up to four to six hours of rituals a day. This behavior was absolutely crippling. My back would hurt so much, my emotions would be out of control, and I lost all gumption to do the things that I enjoyed to do.

To give you a small idea of some of the rituals I performed:

- I had to walk over every crack in the street and every dividing line, visible or not, on the floors, in houses, and everywhere with my left foot first. My mind would even start to calculate from about thirty steps away which foot would eventually cross first, so I could make the necessary adjustments. I was amazed at how accurate my mind was in calculating the distance.

- I had to make sure that every movable thing in my room was on a forty-five degree angle.

- I had to save things that I knew I would never use, basically, just garbage. Used deodorant containers, pieces of paper, empty water bottles, etc.

- I had to keep checking the stove, locks, toaster, car doors, and anything that was electrical.

- I counted practically everything around me. As soon as I walked into a room, I counted the number of people in it. I counted furniture, windows, pictures, and decorations. Every time I was in a car, I counted passing cars, telephone poles, birds, and even waves in the ocean. I counted each step I walked up or down a flight of stairs. I also counted the seconds it took me to close the door, change the channel on the TV, and wash my hands.

- If I picked up anything, I had to tap on it a certain number of times and wave two fingers over the top in a particular motion.

I could write page after page of the rituals I performed in order to relax my mind and to rid the crippling pain of anxiety. If you would like to read more on my rituals, you can check out my previous book, *The Power of the Mind: How I Beat OCD*.

Not only was this suffering taking over my life, it was becoming my life. I had no idea what to do and no idea where to turn. My family wanted to help so much. But I never wanted to talk about something that I could not explain.

In grade twelve, my life shifted when a friend handed me a magazine. In this magazine was a girl's story of her constant anxiety. What swept me off my feet was her story of the rituals she did to relieve her anxiety. Her rituals were the same rituals I did! I literally couldn't believe it. As I continued to read her story, I truly thought I was dreaming. I didn't think anyone else on earth was going through what I was going through. She finished the article by explaining that what she was experiencing and was diagnosed with was Obsessive Compulsive Disorder. It was the first time that my eyes saw these three words together.

From that day forward, I decided that I needed to know everything I possibly could about OCD. I then, somewhere inside of me, found the courage to reach out to my father and inform him that I needed help; one of the hardest things I've ever done. After being formally diagnosed with a very severe case of Obsessive Compulsive Disorder and depression, I made it a mission to not allow this disorder to control my life. By implementing what you are about to read in this book, I stuck to that challenge and now live a life of peace, harmony, and gratitude.

It has been almost fifteen years since then. What I learned throughout that struggle is priceless to me. I've learned truths that have truly changed my life. I have seen recovery of thousands of people all over the world where recovery was not believed possible. I have learned that there are many modalities of medicine that I didn't know existed before. More than anything, I have learned the absolute astonishing power of the human mind.

By using the information provided in the following chapters, I changed my life.

Chapter 3

Let's start to question what we know about anxiety.

You may experience anxiety on a daily basis or you may have the occasional bout of it. Your palms may sweat; you may feel sick to your stomach, have obsessive thoughts, or not be able to be around people. These are all symptoms of anxiety. But how do we tend to look at anxiety? We most certainly don't give it thanks. Why would we give something thanks if it's causing us pain, agony, and discomfort? Well, it's my hope and goal in this book to change your perspective and open your eyes to what anxiety truly is.

Imagine breaking your leg but not having the ability to feel the pain associated with the broken leg. What would you do? You would continue to walk on that leg until you permanently damaged it. The pain is a defense mechanism created by the brain to send you a warning signal (called physical pain), to tell you to take action—it's telling you to get to the nearest hospital and get it addressed. Without the sense of physical pain, you wouldn't have the ability to know when you're facing a physical problem. Imagine that you're cooking and you accidentally stick your hand on the hot burner while you are preoccupied with watching something on television. What would you do if you didn't have the ability to feel the pain associated with the hot burner? You would continue to keep your hand there until you permanently damaged it. The physical pain is a warning sign that is sent to your hand as physical pain, telling you to get your hand off that hot burner before you do permanent damage to it.

Physical pain is our friend. It is a brilliant defense mechanism that was created to tell us that we need to address something (stop walking on the broken leg or remove our hand from the hot burner). The sensation of pain works at lightning fast speed to send us a warning signal to take action now. Without the ability to feel physical pain, we would be in a worse state than when we are experiencing physical pain.

Anxiety works in the same way as physical pain. It is a defense mechanism created by the brain to send warning signals that something is off balance in our lives, whether that is stress from financial strain, relationship issues, or problems with the children. Anxiety is psychological pain that is created to tell us that something has to be addressed. It's a friend. It's a warning sign. It's a defense mechanism.

Imagine that you're out swimming in a lake when an alligator slowly sneaks up within feet of you, ready to pounce on you. If your brain didn't kick in and make you feel the flight or fight response (heart racing, tensing up, increased strength), you become the alligator's dinner. But your brain goes into action and works in your favor, telling you to get the heck out of there before you become alligator food. This experience is a warning sign sent to us in the form of anxiety.

Simply put, physical pain is a warning sign that something has to be addressed physically; anxiety is a warning sign that something has to be addressed psychologically.

You're probably now saying, *"But Jeremy, I experience anxiety every day and there are no alligators, bears, or lions trying to eat me. In fact, I am in absolutely no danger at all. Why do I still have anxiety?"* Well, the reality is this. Anxiety is a defense mechanism that is created over time that sends warning signals to warn you of the toxic behaviour and thoughts that you are having on a regular basis. After dealing with so much stress associated with your financial situation, problems with your kids, marriage issues, or whatever is causing you to experience discomfort, it will eventually get the best of you, if you are not dealing with it in an effective way. How does it get the best of you? It creates warning signs: anxiety attacks, obsessive worrying, etc. This anxiety is the brain's way of sending a warning signal to say, "Address it!"

When you break your arm, what do you do? You go to the hospital right away to have it addressed. When you burn your hand, what do you do? You get it addressed in whatever way that may be. But what happens when you experience anxiety? Do you get it addressed? Do you try to find the cause? Do you look at your life and question what could possibly be causing the anxiety? What do you tend to do when you experience anxiety? I bet you hate it. I bet you curse it. I bet you complain about it afterwards and even during the process, don't you? Well, what is that doing to your anxiety? You're actually making it worse, so much worse.

CHAPTER 3   **Let's start to question what we know about anxiety.**

Right now do a little experiment. Put all your attention, focus, and energy on your feet. While you are doing this, you are going to start to feel your feet tingle; maybe you'll feel a little warmth to your feet or maybe coolness. You're going to start to feel your feet in some capacity. When you start to feel your feet, ask yourself a question. "Why didn't I feel my feet five minutes ago?" You didn't feel your feet five minutes ago because you were not thinking about your feet. Energy flows where your thoughts are. So what's my point? What happens when you are experiencing a headache or any kind of physical pain and you start to complain about it? You will inevitably make the headache worse. You will amplify the pain every single time. You amplify it by bringing negative attention to it. The same holds true for anxiety. The second you give negative attention to it by hating it, cursing it, or complaining about it, you will always make it worse.

Anxiety is a warning sign sent to you as a gift, as a friend, to tell you that something has to be addressed. Without the gift of anxiety, the issues causing you the stress would eventually take over and cause you more harm than you can imagine. Anxiety steps in to say, "Address it!"

Imagine being in your house when your friend walks in. He suddenly shouts out, "Oh my God! You have a huge cut on your forehead! Hurry and get in my car! You have to go get stitches. You're bleeding way too much!" Imagine your reaction being, "Shut up! Mind your own business!" How would your friend react? He would react with hostility. Your friend saw that something was wrong (the blood pouring out of your head), tried to help by sending a warning sign (telling you to get help), and you reacted with hostility saying that you don't need help. This would upset your friend and he would act in accordance to the same energy you supplied him with, negative energy!

Well, anxiety is that friend. It is sent to you as a friend, a warning sign, and a defense mechanism, to tell you that something has to be addressed. When you greet it with hatred, anger, and hostility, it reacts by creating more anxiety. You get exactly what you put out.

We need to change our perception of anxiety. It is not a bad thing. I am not saying that while experiencing it, it doesn't feel bad. It feels terrible. But so does physical pain. But without either "friend," we would be in a worse state than what we go through when we experience both. We need to learn to embrace it, just like we embrace physical pain. This is a crucial element in dealing with anxiety.

Start to replace "hating" with "trying to understand" what's going on in your life to cause it. It's sent to you for this reason. Accept why it's in your life and then address it.

It is important to note that this book concentrates on the causes of anxiety and how to prevent it from occurring. Many people seek a "quick fix" and want to know how to stop a panic attack. This book does not concentrate on how to stop a panic attack, once you are in the midst of one. It concentrates on showing you how to prevent them from happening all together. The goal of this book is to help bring you to a place where panic attacks are no longer taking over your life and no longer occurring. Having a quick fix to stop a panic attack will never treat the cause of why they are occurring and therefore panic attacks will continue to take place. It should be your goal to eliminate them as opposed to merely stop them when they happen. This book is designed to give you the tools to do that.

Read on to understand where it's coming from and more importantly to learn how you (yes, you) are creating it.

Chapter 4

You cannot heal by pointing fingers.

Are you experiencing anxiety, stress, or depression because of something that you experienced in the past? Did you go through something at one point in your life that you are now reliving in your mind? Is the agony of sexual abuse, an unfaithful marriage, or a death causing you to experience a life full of discomfort, anxiety, or depression?

There is something crucial we must understand while trying to tackle anxiety, stress, or depression. The crucial element is this:

No situation or person in your life can cause you to experience anxiety, stress, or depression. You may be thinking, "No, Jeremy, you're wrong. I was abused ten years ago and I am still suffering with anxiety because of the repercussions of the experience." Or maybe you're thinking, "I am stressed out because of my work load that I experience every day." Maybe you're thinking, "I caught my spouse cheating and now I am going through a great deal of stress because of this revelation."

CHAPTER 4 You cannot heal by pointing fingers.

Well, even though these situations are very traumatic experiences, they are not causing you to experience anxiety, stress, or depression. Then what is causing you to experience these elements of discomfort? It's never the situation that causes you to experience anxiety, stress, or depression; it is your psychological *reaction* to these situations.

It's never the *situation*; it's your *reaction* to the situation. Why is this important? This is crucial to understand because the situation that you experienced in the past cannot change, but your reaction to it can. If you continue to point fingers at the situation and blame it for what you are now experiencing, you are putting all the responsibility on the situation. The situation is never going to change. So if you're putting blame on the situation for the anxiety and that situation is never going to change (because it's in the past), guess what, you are not going to break through the tight hold of anxiety, stress, and depression.

It's difficult to sit back and realize this truth. But it is this truth that can liberate you beyond words. Most people go through life blaming some situation or person for the discomfort they are experiencing. They want the situation or person to change because they believe this will be the healing of their anxiety. But the reality is the ego (which I will talk about later) will just find another situation or person to influence them, causing stress or anxiety.

If situations actually caused stress, then every person in the world would react to the same situation in the exact same way. We know this is simply not true. How can one person be scared of a spider while another person loves to work in an insectarium? How can some people love roller coasters and others are terrified? How can one person love to hang out with a particular person while another person despises that person? How can some people love scary movies, while others cover their eyes? It's because situations don't cause us to feel certain feelings; it's our thoughts about the situations causing us to experience what we do. Situations do not cause the stress. Our thoughts about the situations cause stress and anxiety.

Let's say, for instance, that you had a wonderful marriage. Your partner treated you with the upmost respect, was open, honest, and loving. Then one day your world shattered when a sudden accident caused their death. Your world tipped upside down and you thought that you would never rebound from this sudden shock. Your kids are experiencing so much pain, agony, and moments of despair. But what we have to realize is that, even though the situation is very traumatic, it is not actually the situation that is causing the despair, sadness, and depression. It is the psychological reaction to the situation causing these negative emotions. I am not saying these emotions should not be experienced. The grieving process is very important. I am just referring to how the emotions are created.

I have a person in my life that is very close to me who had lost his father. One day, a couple of months after the death, we went rock climbing indoors. When he was fifteen feet above the floor, hanging onto the rocks, he, for one of the first times since the death of his father, felt as though he was experiencing peace.

He later told me that when he was fifteen feet above the ground, looking down and concentrating his every movement on not falling, he felt as though he was not experiencing reality because he was not sad for those brief moments. But what he failed to understand is that he was experiencing reality in its entirety. He was experiencing the present moment. We will discuss the present moment in great detail throughout this book. For those brief moments, he was experiencing life without thinking. He was in the now. He was still. He was in a meditation. He was healing.

Anxiety arrives by dwelling on negative things that happened in the past, or by fearing what could potentially happen in the future. By concentrating on what is going on right at this moment, the mind is calmed and the mind is still. We will discuss this as the chapters move on.

As difficult as this is to digest, we are the creators of our own anxiety, stress, and depression. In order to heal and recover through anxiety, we have to take full responsibility for it and stop pointing fingers at other people or situations. If we continue to blame, we cannot heal. If we continue to point fingers, we are not taking responsibility for something that we are creating ourselves.

Imagine that you worked on your garden, day in and day out for several weeks. It was the most beautiful garden in town. Many bright exotic plants were streaming with life. As everyone passed your house in their vehicle, they would slow down or stop on the side of the road simply to gaze at the beauty. Well, after the work you put into your garden, the sweat, dedication, and commitment, would you then turn around and say you had nothing to do with the garden and that your neighbor created it all? Of course you wouldn't.

Well, why would you blame someone else for something that you are creating yourself? You cannot solve the problem without getting to the root of the problem. You.

Situations cannot cause anxiety. Your reaction to the situations causes anxiety. You have to change. How? The rest of the book is dedicated to showing you what you have to do.

Read on.

Chapter 5

Addressing the cause.

It is very important to realize there are qualified professionals out there who have amazing abilities to help people suffering from anxiety. There are well-trained psychologists, counsellors, therapists, etc. that can work wonders for sufferers of anxiety. I share what has worked for me, the science of how the mind/brain works in relation to our daily activities, and how to rest the mind in practical ways; ways that work.

One of the most important steps you can take while dealing with anxiety is reaching out to someone, whether that person be a doctor, psychologist, or simply someone you trust. The first step, before all others, should be reaching out for help.

Considering this, I'd like to share with you what I have learned during my time of suffering with anxiety, but even more so what I have learned after overcoming something I thought I would never overcome.

Not only do many anxiety sufferers think they are the only ones who understand the severity of what they're going through, but they also believe their anxiety or depression magically appeared out of nowhere. But the reality of the situation is that there is no mystical anxiety creature out there, preying upon the weak by sticking the "anxiety chemical" into their brains to gradually sink into their sixty trillion cells.

Everything we suffer from in life has to have a cause. Why does your foot hurt? Maybe it is because you accidentally banged it on the leg of the sofa. Why do you have a headache? Maybe you are dehydrated. Why are you tired? Maybe it is because you had only four hours of sleep the night before. Just like Newton said, "For every effect there has to be a cause." But many anxiety sufferers believe there is *no* cause to their anxiety and that they have been cursed with it.

Knowing that there is indeed a cause to your anxiety is the first step in realizing that you can actually do something about it.

Although there are aspects of our medical system doing wonders for people suffering with health deficiencies here in the western world, a lot of the time our medical system does more harm than good. I am certainly not downgrading our medical system. We have amazing physicians and health care professionals that are great in emergencies, but a lot of the time when faced with anxiety, western medicine tends to make the matter worse.

Most of the time, the cause of the anxiety is not addressed. In millions of situations, sufferers of anxiety visit the doctor only to be prescribed an anti-depressant/anxiety medication. What

CHAPTER 5 **Addressing the cause.**

is this doing? It is masking the pain of anxiety and depression. It never treats what's actually causing the anxiety/depression. How can someone expect to be healed from anxiety/depression, if they are not doing anything about the cause of where it's coming from? For some, medication is absolutely needed, not only anti-depressants, but also other forms as well. But when medication is prescribed without looking into any alternatives, alternatives that could very much be more beneficial, then it is time to ask questions.

Imagine entering the emergency room with a bone sticking out of your leg, and blood gushing out of the wound, causing excruciating pain beyond anything you've ever experienced. The doctor looks at you and says, "This should be an easy fix. I'll give you a painkiller for the pain. It should take care of the issue and you'll be fixed up within a few weeks." And you say, "What about the bone sticking out of my leg, since that is the actual reason why I am hurting?" Well, luckily the doctor would never only give you a painkiller. They would address the cause and do their best to reset the bone, allowing nature to heal the wound.

But what happens when you take a medication to aid in the recovery of anxiety and neglect to do anything else to eliminate the cause? You are only masking the pain and you are not treating the cause. You are not experiencing anxiety or depression because you have an anti-depressant deficiency. We need to learn to treat the cause.

Sometimes, medication is absolutely needed. Pharmaceuticals definitely have a place in this world and do a lot of good in certain situations. But the sad reality is that pharmaceuticals are massively abused and mass marketed to millions of vulnerable sufferers. Pharmaceutical companies are "for profit" companies. If they didn't make money, they wouldn't survive. Their main interest is money, not health. This is important to understand.

So many times, the very first form of treatment for anxiety is a pharmaceutical drug. This is ludicrous. Sometimes pharmaceuticals are the right choice, but it is vital to address the cause of the suffering. If you are currently taking medication, do not stop the medication without talking to your doctor. Stopping any form of medication abruptly can do more harm than good. It is crucial to talk to your doctor before changing your medication regimen.

So now, you're asking, "Okay, anxiety has a cause. What is it?" Most people are looking for one big, traumatic event they experienced as a child or throughout their lifetime that caused their anxiety. I have talked to thousands of people in my career and noticed it is very rarely that. But the dozens of little things we do on a daily basis is actually contributing to the anxiety. For example, it is not the one greasy meal you had six months ago that caused you to gain an extra twenty pounds. The sodas, unnecessary sugar, and late night snacks that you consumed on a daily basis caused you to gain the extra weight. Most people are completely oblivious as to what they are doing to cause anxiety.

In fact, so many people blame anxiety on genetics and heredity. We have known since the 1970s, hereditary actually plays a much smaller role than initially thought in the development of disease. When it comes to certain illnesses, yes, we may inherit the particular genes from our parents. Whether or not those genes are activated boils down to the lifestyle we live and what we eat. But more important than any other factor is what we hold predominately in our subconscious mind. This book is about demystifying anxiety and showing you where it truly comes from. But more importantly, this book is about showing you how to live a life of peace, harmony, and balance, free of unneeded stress, anxiety, and depression. If you are willing to do the work, do the techniques described, and really dedicate yourself to improving your life, then you can actually transform your life in a way that you never thought was possible.

Chapter 6

When we were babies.

Can you imagine what it's like to be a baby again? You were so content with the way the world worked.

You laughed when you felt like it and cried when things didn't go your way. You never held grudges against people. You didn't judge others upon their actions and didn't ridicule or think differently of them when they did "wrong." You walked around next to your mother and father and were amazed by your surroundings. Everything around you was an adventure because you didn't know what it was all about. You had an urge to touch everything, play with things, and explore.

Your friends would come over to play with you. Sometimes you would like it and sometimes you wouldn't. At times, you wanted to share and other times you didn't. But never did you hold a grudge as a baby. You never grabbed toys from your friend's hands because you thought they didn't "deserve" to play with them or that they weren't good enough. You showed your true feelings every minute without caring what your mother or father would think of you.

CHAPTER 6 **When we were babies.**

You didn't care what you wore as long as it was comfortable. You didn't care about the spaghetti in your hair unless it dripped down your forehead and dried up in the corner of your eye. You didn't care if anyone smelled a foul odor that slowly crept into the room made by a particular part of your body, or the sound made when the odor was released. You played with your toys and left them behind on the floor wherever you happened to be sitting. You didn't care if those around you thought you were lazy because you didn't put your toys back in the play area.

You didn't care if anyone thought you were grumpy, shy, or overweight. You didn't care about calories and were not concerned about what you were going to do Friday night. You didn't dwell on the fact that your baby friend broke your toy the day before or if he was going to do that to another toy the next day.

What was it like to be a baby? What was it like not to care about how you looked or how others perceived you? What was it like to not be concerned about how respected your line of work was, how much money you made, or your social class? What was it like to live day by day in the present moment, not dwelling on the bad that happened the week before, or the bad that could happen the week after?

When we were babies, we were so pure, innocent, and loved life. We didn't have expectations of good or bad and didn't judge others based upon anything they did. We lived completely in the moment. We appreciated when good presented itself in our lives and cried when we were hurt. We were so completely absorbed in exactly what was going on at the time that we didn't care about anything else. We ate when we were hungry, used the bathroom when we felt like it, and fell asleep when we were tired, even if Mom was in our face "baby talking" to us.

Life was wonderful. Life was perfect. But something happened as we started to grow. It would taunt us for the rest of our lives, controlling our actions, and causing us to change ourselves just to please others. It was something so powerful that it would cause our self-esteem to lower, creating stress and anxiety. It caused us to hate ourselves and constantly adjust whom we truly are, trying to reach and achieve what everyone else had, just to feel good about ourselves.

We started to be brainwashed by the lies of humanity.

We started to "think" and become possessed by the "ego."

The ego

We are all born into this world with a mind that is so pure, so clean, and so innocent. As babies, we laugh and cry when we feel like it. We don't care what others think about us and don't allow them to influence our decisions. We don't dwell on negative things in the past and don't fear things that could happen in the future. We are so present and so still.

But as we start to progress in age, our minds start to develop and form beliefs about the world, people, and most importantly ourselves. Most of these beliefs are lies. Some of these lies are:

We have to be a particular size/figure in order to be happy.

We have to wear brand name clothes in order to be "cool."

We need to get high marks in school in order to "be somebody" when we get older.

We need to make lots of money because money buys happiness.

We need to look like the Hollywood stars in order to be recognized.

These "lies" are just the tip of the iceberg. As we continue to be fed these beliefs, we start to allow them to interfere with our free will and our happiness. We start to shape our lives around these beliefs to the point where unnecessary stress consumes our lives. This stress then lowers our confidence level. And once we realize that we can't obtain the "perfect life," we become depressed.

All these "lies" are work of what is called the "ego" or "false self."

Humans are born into this world perfect. But when we allow the ego to severely control our lives, we are living in a state of "Hell on Earth." When we learn to not only recognize the ego but also control it, we begin to live a blissful life free of unnecessary suffering.

Jesus said, "The Kingdom of Heaven is within you." But we are constantly searching outside of us to find this Kingdom. We don't need to "find" anything in order to obtain Heaven. We actually have to "let go" of our "false self" (the ego). Buddha said, "All that you are is the result of what you have thought." Jesus also said, "I assure you that unless you change and become like little children, you cannot enter the Kingdom of Heaven."

In my opinion, that's what Jesus meant when he said, "The Kingdom of Heaven is within you."

When we learn to become pure of mind, pure of heart, and control our ego, then we obtain Heaven on Earth. Babies' minds are in a state of peace, harmony, and completely free of "unnecessary" stress and suffering. Adults can achieve this state as well.

In Buddhism, this state is called Nirvana and "I" believe this is Jesus' message of Heaven on Earth. The following sections will show you how to find that Heaven on earth.

Chapter 7

The Powerhouse to your everything.

Now that we realize "we" create our own stress and anxiety and that situations cannot cause you to experience it, we need to now look at the astonishing power of thoughts. But before getting into the dozens of little things we do on a daily basis that actually contributes to creating stress and anxiety, we need to understand, at least a little, how the brain and mind works.

The Subconscious Mind: The Powerhouse to who we are.

My intention is for this book to show you the practical side of human nature, and what it is doing to our health. Even so, I cannot ignore one of the most important elements in all healing, and where it comes from. What I am about to disclose in this chapter deals with something called the subconscious mind. Maybe this is a subject that you are well versed in or maybe it's something you know nothing about. I am going to try my best not to get too "sciencey" and show you the main functions of your subconscious mind, how important it is to our health, why this is the powerhouse to who we are, what shapes it, and how to change it.

What is the subconscious mind?

Ask yourself right now; what is controlling the flow of your blood? What is, while you're sitting down right now reading these words, commanding your blood to flow at a particular speed and pressure against your arteries? When you swallow your food, do you tell your esophagus to perform particular rhythmic motions to force that food into your stomach? What's making your heart beat right now? How does your fingernail grow?

The human body is made up of anywhere between sixty-one hundred trillion cells. Each and every single cell is doing hundreds of thousands of actions every single second. And every single cell knows exactly what every other cell is doing the second it does it.

Where is this intelligence coming from? It's coming from something called the subconscious mind.

Let's break down the subconscious. *Sub* means below and *conscious* means your awareness. So, subconscious means *below your awareness*. If your subconscious mind is below your conscious mind, well, what is the conscious mind?

Your conscious mind is the part of your mind that is aware of your surroundings. The conscious mind is the mind of your five senses: smell, taste, touch, hearing, and sight. It's the part of your mind that allows you to experience the physical world through your five senses. It's also the part of your mind that reasons. It registers and remembers the things that you are exposed to.

CHAPTER 7   **The Powerhouse to your everything.**

Imagine if you're walking in downtown New York City on a snowy day. You can feel the snow crunch under your shoes. You can smell the fresh bread being made from the bakery a hundred feet away. You can hear the conversations of the people around, and you can see the bright blue sky over your head. Every single bit of information that goes into either one of your five senses is called a bit of information (BOI). You can consciously be aware of approximately 2,000 bits per second. These are the things that you are aware of entering your mind. When you are aware of what you smell, that means you're registering what you smell, which means that it is entering your conscious mind. When you see your dream-car zoom down the street and you refer to it in your mind that means you are aware it's there and you are registering it. What about the hundreds of cars you are seeing but not registering? What about all the other smells that are going into your nose that you are not aware of? What about all the conversations you are hearing but not paying attention to? What about all the other sources of information going into your five senses that you are not noticing? Since it is going into your senses, where is it going? It's going into your subconscious mind, where it is stored and most certainly not forgotten. Your conscious mind can register approximately 2,000 bits per second, whereas your subconscious mind can register over 400 billion bits of information per second. Read that again. Over 400 billion bits of information per second are registered. Absolutely everything that you see, taste, feel, hear, and smell is being recorded in your subconscious mind.

Here's what you need to remember:

Your conscious mind is the part of your mind that deals with the things that are going on right now, in this moment. It's

53

what you're paying attention to right now. Your subconscious mind deals with much more important things in your life. It deals with your personality, values, what inspires you, and your fundamental beliefs. How you tend to react to situations is determined by what you are holding in your subconscious mind.

For instance, if you have the belief that you do not have what it takes to lose ten pounds, you can say consciously all you want that you're going to lose the weight, but your subconscious mind will win and create a reality in accordance to it. In fact, researchers are telling us that over 95% of the time our desires, cravings, urges, and decisions are made in accordance to whatever our subconscious mind holds. What your subconscious mind holds as a belief becomes your reality. That's why willpower doesn't work out in our favor. If you're on a diet and trying to stay away from cupcakes, your conscious mind, which is where your willpower comes from, will only work for you 2-4% of the time. So, for the few first days you may be able to stay away. But before you know it, your subconscious mind kicks in and wins the battle, forcing you to eat what you are trying to stay away from.

We need to learn to address the beliefs in our subconscious mind. This part controls who we are and what we are attracted to. This book will address how subconscious beliefs are formed, but more importantly, how to change them.

Chapter 8

The most important part of this book! It doesn't know the difference!

When I say that you create your own stress and anxiety, I mean it. And now, I want to show you how you do that. If you're going to take one thing away from this entire book, let it be this statement: Your mind does not know the difference between something that's actually happening and when you merely imagine something. Your brain and body react in the same exact way.

Think about what happens when you awake from a nightmare. Your mind is racing; you're sweating; and you're anxious beyond words. Your body reacted as if it was really in danger. But you weren't. So why would your body react in such a way if you were never in danger to begin with, and if the nightmare was merely in your mind? It's because your mind does not know the difference between something real and something imagined.

Imagine something very traumatic that has triggered a lot of stress in your life. Let's say that your spouse was cheating on you. Even though this may have happened years ago, the thought of it makes you sick to your stomach, your heart beats fast, and it fuels you with jealousy and anger. But you have to realize what is happening. It's not what happened years ago that is making you feel the discomfort, it's your thoughts about it.

This has been demonstrated time and again with the placebo effect. The placebo effect takes place when you have two groups of subjects suffering from the same illness. Group A is given a pharmaceutical drug that is designed to address their illness. Group B gets a sugar pill (thinking it's a pharmaceutical drug designed to address the illness). But amazingly both report relief of the symptoms. How? It's because when the mind holds a particular belief, the brain reacts as if that belief is reality, whether it is or not.

There is also something call the nocebo effect. With the nocebo effect, the mind actually convinces the body that it has an illness. Consider a hypochondriac. A hypochondriac is someone that hears about an illness, and then is convinced they actually have it, when they do not. They start to experience the symptoms because their mind is convincing them they have the illness. Whatever the mind holds as a belief, the body reacts to.

A multitude of things we do on a daily basis contributes to the development of stress, anxiety, and depression. In the next chapter, we will explore the top things (in my opinion) that contribute to stress and anxiety. Remember, it's rarely the one big, traumatic experience causing your anxiety. It's the many things you are doing on a daily basis that's actually creating it. Read on to see what is actually causing what you are going through.

Chapter 9

Top things that contribute to stress and anxiety.

A lot of people think it's one big, traumatic experience that causes prolonged anxiety, but most are not willing to see the daily things that actually create it. It's like a person who cannot seem to lose weight saying, "I don't eat big, greasy meals," but he neglects to see the extra fatty condiments being added to his food, the sodas, and the snacks before bed that actually contribute to his weight gain.

So much of the time, it's the little things we do on a daily basis that actually add up and create the anxiety we are going through. It's not the one big thing, but the many, many little things that change brain chemistry and create stress and anxiety.

Here are the most significant things people do on a daily basis that not only weaken their immune system but actually create stress and anxiety.

Complaining

Several things happen when a person complains. Imagine being in a stressful situation and doing something that takes your mind off of it. For that hour, you feel great, rejuvenated, alive, and peaceful. But once you start thinking about the situation, you feel the stress all over again. Remember, it's never the situation that is causing you stress, it is your psychological reaction (thoughts) about the situation that cause you to experience stress and anxiety.

When someone complains, it is a reminder of a person or situation that is triggering stress and anxiety. Every time they complain, a part of their brain called the hypothalamus triggers the release of a chemical called cortisol from the adrenal gland in the kidneys. This chemical has several negative effects on the body:

- It produces stress.

- Creates anxiety.

- Can lead you down a road to depression, depending on how much you release on a daily basis.

- It weakens your immune system.

- Disrupts sleep.

- Raises blood pressure.

- Makes you gain weight.

- Breaks down muscle, bone, and connective tissue.

- Plus, many more negative side effects.

CHAPTER 9   Top things that contribute to stress and anxiety.

Note that in certain situations cortisol release is great. If an alligator is chasing you, you want to release cortisol, as it's the stress response. It gives you a quick burst of energy, lowers your sensitivity to pain, and gets you out of the way of the alligator. But most times, the release of cortisol is due to negative thoughts. This type of cortisol release is doing nothing but negative things on the body. It's destroying it, in fact.

Let's take the weather as an example. Did you know that it is scientifically impossible for the weather to be bad? How can weather be good or bad? Weather is exactly as it is. Our perception of the weather makes us "feel" bad about it. Imagine you wake up on a cold winter's day to look outside at a huge storm. A huge amount of snow is falling and the city is practically shut down for the day. Most people would hate this and not hesitate a second to start complaining. What about the manager of the ski lodge that lives five miles away from you? Does he complain? No, he rejoices because for the past two months they have not had enough snow to open the ski slopes. Because of his attitude, his brain releases endorphins, the good-feeling chemical.

We have to realize that situations are not good or bad. Situations are exactly that, situations. They cannot cause you stress or anxiety. It's absolutely impossible. Our psychological reaction to a situation causes us stress or anxiety. This is one of the biggest myths of dealing with anxiety and stress. We need to stop blaming other people and situations for the negativity that we create in our own lives.

It is also important to note that admitting and talking about a fact may not be complaining. If a situation or a "wrong"

59

that someone did is brought up to address an issue, this is not necessarily complaining. Complaining occurs when you needlessly bring up something that you are discontent with, just to bring it up. It is not brought up to be proactive, to resolve, or to address somehow. It is just brought up to simply complain. This destroys the body.

Always remember there are millions of people in this world that would do anything to have the ability to complain about your "problems." We are so spoiled in the western world. There are millions upon millions of people starving, homeless, and have absolutely no family to call their own. Yet, we in the first world complain about our problems, when the reality is most of these "problems" are not only not problems, but are certainly not something that we should complain about.

Take for example, complaining when stuck in traffic. Have you ever done this? Instead of complaining about being stuck in traffic, be thankful you have a vehicle that you can drive to work. Do you realize how many people in this world not only do not have a vehicle but also don't have shoes to wear? Do you ever complain about your kids? Sure you do. Do you know how lucky you are that you are blessed with the gift of children? Millions of people, who do not have this ability, would do anything to be in your position right now. Do you ever complain about your job? Around the world, millions of people without jobs would do anything for the opportunity to work and be paid.

We need to switch our perspective. You don't have to work; you *get* to work. You don't have to take care of your kids. You *get* to take care of your kids. You don't have to drive to work and get stuck in traffic, you *get* to drive to work and get stuck in traffic. First world problems are not problems.

Complaining triggers the release of cortisol, which then not only weakens your immune system, but also actually creates stress and anxiety.

Buddha said, "You will not be punished for your anger. You will be punished by your anger."

You cannot be grateful and complain at the same time. Choose being grateful.

Gossiping

Every time that you gossip, you hold a negative thought about a person. "Did you hear who she slept with?" "Did you hear what he did to his wife?" Every time that you gossip, you hold negative thoughts in your mind and you vocalize these negative thoughts. Remember, every negative thought has a vibrational frequency. These vibrational frequencies either heighten or lower the effectiveness of your immune system. In this case, gossiping lowers your immune system. Gossiping is a form of complaining in disguise. Also, when you gossip, you feel this artificial sense of temporary power. This power comes in the form of, "I know something that you don't know." This power is the ego wanting to be superior to the person that you are gossiping to. When the ego is activated, it always grows.

Also, the person that you are gossiping to typically loves the juicy information you are telling them. Then, they feel superior to the other people in their circle of friends that do not know the information. This not only grows their ego but also gives them the ability to gossip about the same subject with a friend, which feeds the vicious cycle of stress and anxiety development.

Every time you gossip, you change the chemistry of your brain, allow the release of cortisol from your adrenal gland, and create stress. You cannot gossip without hurting yourself.

It's the little things that we do on a daily basis that is actually contributing to what we thought one big event was creating. We need to start considering all the little things.

Judging

When you judge you think, "I am better than you because I would never do what you did." Well, the reality is, if you were raised in exactly the same way as that person, was exposed to exactly the same things that person was exposed to, had the same exact thoughts that person had, then yes, you would do exactly the same thing. In order to judge a person, you have to hold negative thoughts in your mind: anger, vengeance, annoyance, envy, etc. All these thoughts destroy your immune system and attack your well-being. You cannot judge without hurting yourself.

Remember that judging is a reflection of how discontent that your mind is. It is a reflection of the person doing the judging, not the person being judged. A peaceful mind cannot judge. A peaceful mind cannot hate. A peaceful mind cannot hold vengeance.

Being materialistic

As we continued to grow older, our thinking mind started to mature. We were introduced to things that made us question life and people. We started to form opinions and allow our parents, siblings, and any other form of authority influence the way we thought about others and ourselves.

Then the lies started to brainwash our innocent mind. We started to think that in order to be appreciated and accepted in life, we had to present ourselves in a certain manner. We had to talk in a particular tone and control our true feelings, even when we felt like crying or laughing out loud. We had to grammatically form our sentences and conduct ourselves "accordingly" to a situation in order to be seen as appropriate. No-name clothing would no longer suffice and brand names became mandatory. Showing up to school in brand-name sneakers and t-shirts made us feel better about ourselves for some reason. We believed that eyeliner, blush, and concealer somehow made us a little better than we were before we put it on our face. We felt as though we had to be great in sports to be accepted or get good grades in order to be seen as a success.

We started to compare our grades and even suffer with fear that the teacher was going to announce the highest mark in the class, knowing it wasn't ours. We didn't want to sit with the un-popular kids on the bus because we were scared that we'd be associated with them. We didn't want to be seen getting picked up after school by our mom or dad, but it wasn't so embarrassing if they had a nice car. We were sometimes scared to invite our girlfriends or boyfriends over for dinner, because our parents weren't as financially successful as our guest, or if they weren't as proper as the married couple down the road.

Life soon became a constant struggle to feel good about ourselves. And how did we do that? We constantly searched for ways to artificially improve our appearance. We strived to obtain the next perfect dress, the next edition of running shoes, and craved to hang out with the popular kids. We had an "image" to protect and we protected it even if it meant jeopardizing our health and wellbeing. Being skinny was more important than being healthy. Being acne free was more important than eating healthy. Having the perfect color hair was more important than sleep. And who you're seen with on the weekends or during lunch hour was more important than the feelings you had towards them.

Then, as we grew older, having nice cars and big trucks became the predominant thoughts in our minds. The Hanna Montana backpacks suddenly turned into $500 Gucci handbags. Having what our friends had was all too important in our lives, and caused us to work overtime hours, just to have enough money to buy what we needed to keep up with them.

As our "toys" became more expensive, the stress and anxiety grew. We needed that next big thing no matter what it took.

CHAPTER 9   Top things that contribute to stress and anxiety.

It felt like a piece of us would be taken away if we couldn't somehow keep up with the neighbors. Our nights of reading to relax ourselves before bed turned into drawing sketches for a swimming pool just a little larger than the one next door. We found ourselves doing courses from online colleges, not to better ourselves, but to have a certain certificate, making us feel a step above a friend.

Life becomes one big competition, even if we are not aware of it.

Would you be happy if you won $50,000? That's such a silly question. Everyone would. But is there a situation where you wouldn't? No, of course not, right?

So many times, I flick on the television and there is a game show on. The player continues to win money, first $1,000, then $2,500, then $10,000, and then $50,000. The person attains the $50,000 and is ecstatic. She is jumping and rolling around on the stage. Tears are falling from her eyes because she just won enough money to pay off her student loan and put her daughter through college. The show continues as her excitement and energy level climbs. She is about to play for $125,000. But if she gets this question wrong, she drops to $50,000 and it's game over. She begins to sweat in anticipation. The host starts to read the question and her shoulders start to sag as she realizes she doesn't know the answer. Time is running out as she ventures a guess. She's wrong. But it's okay because she's leaving with $50,000 right? Wrong. The anguish of disappointment completely destroys her ability to smile. She slowly walks over to the host of the show and almost regretfully accepts her $50,000 check.

How could she possibly be disappointed? She just won $50,000! The answer is that she compared it to what could have happened. She could have won $125,000, if she guessed the correct answer. But she didn't, so she only won $50,000. She made a direct comparison to what she had to what she could have had. The second we make a comparison of what we could have, we realize what we don't have, and it causes us to become sad.

Would you be happy if you just won $500 out of nowhere? Of course, you would. But imagine hearing someone knocking at your door. You answer the door to see a camera crew and a gentlemen with a jumbo check for $1,000,000 written out to you. You would jump through the roof with excitement. But think about the person holding the check getting a phone call from his producer, and saying that there was a huge mistake. They had the wrong address, but as a consolation prize, they gave you $500. How would you feel? You would feel like a) punching him; b) kicking him; or c) crying until you drove them away. Why? Because you compared the situation to what you could have had. You didn't have the $1,000,000 to begin with. It was a mistake. So, you have $500 in your hands that you did not have ten minutes prior to them arriving. It was $500 in your hands, a gift. But still you feel sad. How can winning $500 make you sad? Because of one reason, you compared it to what you could have had and did not appreciate what you had now.

Comparison can be a demon.

We live in a society that believes material things will bring us happiness, when, in fact, they do the complete opposite. I am not saying that you should never enjoy buying a nice dress, car, or something that you enjoy. That is fine. But we need to realize happiness cannot come from anything that you purchase or acquire. It is impossible. Happiness is a state of mind. Happiness occurs when you are experiencing peacefulness, tranquility, and presence. Happiness occurs in a person who is well balanced and is awakened to life as it truly is.

You are probably asking yourself why you feel great after buying a new car, house, or dress. Well, the happiness you feel is just an illusion. Nothing that you can buy can create happiness. Remember, it is always your thoughts about things that create sadness or happiness. You still may be saying, "I disagree. My job makes me happy. My new car makes me happy. My new dress makes me happy." This is the illusion. One thing you will notice is that the happiness feeling when you purchase something new will eventually wither away. The reason why you feel happy when you buy something is that all your attention is then put on the new thing, whether that is a new car, boat, or even a girlfriend or boyfriend. If all or most of your attention is put on the new thing/person, then that's less time put on all the things that you typically complain about, dwell on, or fear. So, in one sense, this process is indeed calming your mind. But you are relying on something external. You will always notice that once the newness of the thing you bought wears out, your regular thinking mind starts to attack you again. All the negative thoughts start to arise and you are back to square one.

What happens next? You start to seek something else to buy, because you know it will come with temporary relief of your agonizing thoughts. You buy something else and once again, your mind is calmed temporarily until that newness of that object fades away. You continue to buy and you continue to feel temporary relief. This becomes a vicious cycle and the cause of your discomfort is never addressed, your negative thoughts.

Alcohol

Imagine that a new drug was introduced to our society, a very addictive drug that affected practically every biological tissue of the body. This drug not only compromises memory and confuses your sense of reality, it also slurs your speech, can make you dizzy, and can leave you completely unconscious. This drug decreases your heart rate, causes extreme sickness, and can even kill you.

This drug is alcohol.

Strip away all the millions of dollars worth of extremely manipulating television and radio commercials done by some of the most sophisticated minds in marketing and look at alcohol for what it truly is. Strip away the illusion of elegance and wine, sports and beer, and all the other traps of these marketing minds. Truly look at what this substance is, a poison that is not designed for human consumption.

Not only does alcohol have huge negative impacts on the physical body, it also has huge impacts on our minds. A lot of people use alcohol to numb the mind so they don't have to deal with whatever is going on in their lives. The second they do this, they give up the opportunity that nature has provided them with (the struggle) to build resilience.

Nature provides us with struggles so that we can effectively overcome them by facing them, getting through them naturally, and then building resilience to face the next struggle so much more effectively.

If you continue to numb your mind with a poison that society does it's best to convince us is "normal," "good," and "social," don't be surprised how your resilience will keep decreasing by every drink and every future struggle will be more difficult to deal with. And seeing that every future struggle will be more difficult, you will be more tempted to drink, which will then make the entire scenario even worse.

Some people may say that alcohol in moderation is all right. But the reality is that is just an excuse to drink. We are simply not designed to ingest a poisonous substance into our bodies.

We have to get past the notion of, "everyone else does it, so it must be okay," in order to see what alcohol is truly doing to our society. We must also get over the notion that just because a substance is legal doesn't mean that it's okay for us to consume.

Many people are attracted to nightclubs. If you want to attract health, happiness, and peace into your life, this is one of the worst places to go. Nightclubs are saturated in a deep, dark, collective consciousness of people that are there to numb their minds, because they are not content with their current life situation. Some people may say they go to dance or to socialize, but let's take the same building, same location, and subtract alcohol from the picture. If they didn't serve alcohol would you continue to go on a regular basis? The reality is, if nightclubs stopped serving alcohol, but continued to have a dance floor and music, those clubs would soon have to close down because people would stop going.

It is very important to sit back and realize why you are attracted to nightclubs and other places that have alcohol as its main attraction. You must ask yourself, why? Questioning this is vital in decreasing anxiety, stress, and even depression.

I present all around the world on how to beat stress, anxiety, and depression. One thing almost everyone I talk to after my presentations has in common is that they drink and/or do recreational drugs to relax. Let's look at alcohol. People drink alcohol, whether or not they want to admit it, because they are somewhat stressed, even on a very minuscule level. The word stressed can be very manipulating. I am not saying that you have to be experiencing anxiety attacks or that you are always tense. I am saying that if you are drinking, you are not completely satisfied with the current moment/situation. When you are not satisfied with something, alcohol helps relax you in a very toxic way. In other words, you are relying on something external to relax you. This will always rob nature's ability to create resilience within you.

You may be saying, "But I only drink when I feel great and celebrate something special." Well, my question back to you is this, "If the situation you are celebrating is so great, then why do you feel the urge to add a toxin to your body and numb your mind?" Remember, the ego can be very, very manipulative. If

CHAPTER 9   Top things that contribute to stress and anxiety.

you're adding a toxin to your body to relax, you are somewhat stressed out or very stressed out. You will notice the people who consume the most alcohol are the people who are the most stressed. So, if you consume a lot of alcohol, it is a complete reflection of how toxic your thoughts are. If you consume a little alcohol, it is still a reflection of how toxic your thoughts are. When you are no longer attracted to alcohol or any toxic substance, it is a reflection of how peaceful the mind is.

If you are attracted to alcohol and look forward to the feeling of being intoxicated (shutting off the mind) even a little bit, it simply means that your mind is not peaceful throughout the day/night. Why else would you crave drinking a poisonous substance? The reason people enjoy alcohol is because it artificially turns off the mind and negative thoughts.

It is important to realize that you are not experiencing stress because you have an alcohol deficiency. If you are experiencing stress for other reasons (which you are), then why would you drink to try to solve the issue? Drinking will only ever make the real cause of your stress grow. It will grow because you are not addressing the cause.

Imagine that you were trying to become a great baseball player. When you play another team that is not as good, you continue to win. Imagine that every single time you faced a team that was much better, you cheated by switching the ball to a cork ball that travels much further when you hit it with the bat. Even though you wouldn't feel the pain of defeat from losing, you would not have the opportunity to grow as a team, because you cheated to numb the pain of yet another loss.

What's going to happen when you have to face another team, that is better than you, but the umpire has caught on to your trick and does not allow you to switch the ball anymore? You're going to lose and probably get thrown out of the league. Then you're going to suffer the punishment of not only losing but also not being able to play again. This is happening because you're not facing the struggle (the better team) the way that you are supposed to, by playing them over and over and getting better at your skill, so the next time you will be much better.

Or imagine that you are training to become a lifeguard but use flippers to practice. How do you build up your leg muscles and endurance so that when you are faced with a real emergency situation, you can swim to rescue the person drowning? The reality is that you can't build it up unless you train without the flippers and work hard, face the training the way that you are supposed to.

Or imagine that you cheated off the person next to you during a first-aid exam. How would you do, during a real life situation where you had to save someone's life? The truth is that they would probably die, if they had to rely on you, because you didn't put the time and effort into studying.

Switching the baseball to play better, using flippers to swim faster, and cheating on an exam is like drinking alcohol to avoid stress. Not only are you not exposing yourself to the pain to build immunity, but also you are numbing the pain artificially. So, the next time you are confronted with the same type of energy, you cannot deal with it as effectively as you would have if you dealt with it naturally to begin with.

And, of course people who consume alcohol are attracted to other people who consume alcohol. In reality, it is people who feel the need to artificially numb the mind that are attracted to other people who feel the need to artificially numb the mind. These people are trying to numb toxic thoughts, so in other words they are stressed. So when you break it down, people who feel the urge to drink are somewhat stressed out or very much stressed out and they attract the same type of people right back into their lives. You will notice that heavy drinkers tend to hang out with heavy drinkers. When this is the case, it's two minds trying to artificially numb toxic thoughts. When one stressful mind attracts another stressful mind, stressful situations typically manifest and the vicious cycle continues.

We are not meant to consume alcohol. Period.

The Illusion of Perfection

When you break it down, what is perfection? How do we measure perfection? Surely, it must exist, if we are always in a state of striving for it in all areas of our lives.

What is the perfect apple? Obviously, in order to measure the perfect apple, you have to compare it to a perfect apple. Where do we find that perfect apple and how would we know when we found it? Apples are comprised of water, fat, protein, carbohydrates, vitamins, and minerals. Most apples are made up of about 90% water. But would we call an apple made up of 80% water imperfect? Typically, a raw apple has about eight milligrams of Vitamin C. But what if we came across one with only five milligrams? Would this make the apple imperfect? Apples typically have about nine milligrams of calcium. But what would happen if we purchased an apple, did analysis on it, and found it contained twelve milligrams of calcium. Would this hinder the apple's ability to obtain that perfection state? Apples typically have about four grams of fiber. What happens to an apple when it only has one gram? Do we throw it out, judge it for not being the norm, and ridicule it? In fact, there are over seven thousand types of apples cultivated all over the world, from braeburn, cameo, and fuji, to gala, honey crisp, and golden delicious. Some of these apples are small, weighing only fifty grams, while others weigh up to a pound. Some of these apples are red, some are yellow, and some are green. Some have dark spots while others are stunningly bright. Some apples are 99% red with a couple of yellowish dots throughout and some are 99% yellow with a few green spots. Some have long stocks and some have short ones. How can we judge a perfect apple when there isn't one particular blueprint of the perfect apple? Every apple is perfect. Every single apple is unique. It would be ridiculous to say to a friend that the apple she is eating is imperfect because it has yellowish spots on it or is a little smaller or bigger in comparison to other apples. So why do we do it with people?

In order to judge others we have to compare them to something. We cannot judge if we are not sticking them alongside of somebody more "perfect" than he or she is. But once again, who would be that perfect being? There is no perfect being out there, because in order to be perfect, you have to have a blueprint of perfection and then create to the perfect measurements, looks, and figure. I don't believe we have a scientist tucked away somewhere in a secret laboratory up in the mountains creating the DNA of humans according to a specific blueprint of what a perfect human should be.

So if my assumption is correct, how could the perfect human even exist? Every human being has one fundamental commonality. We are conscious beings having a human experience. All the things we judge in others are elements of the person that we think are not perfect. But once again, what is that perfect being? We can't compare anyone to the perfect being because we don't have a blueprint of the perfect being. It just does not exist.

We can talk about a baseball diamond being perfect, as it is molded off a particular blueprint of what a perfect baseball diamond should look like. The field itself has to follow its blueprint precisely in order to work efficiently. It has to have adequate water drainage with proper design, installed and maintained irrigation systems, and the necessary maintenance program to address unexpected clay conditions due to weather. Measurement of the distance between bases has to be precise, creating a perfect diamond. The position from home plate to second base has to be about one hundred and twenty-seven feet, while the space between each base is about ninety feet, leaving the pitcher's mound to home plate about sixty and a half feet. The top of the mound has to consist of a plateau that is about five feet wide, while the diameter of the mound is about eighteen feet. Given the hundreds of other tedious measurements to create the fence, bleachers, dugouts, batters boxes, etc., the construction workers depend on a blueprint to create something very similar to the original.

But human beings don't have a blueprint. Like I mentioned previously, there is no mad scientist hiding away creating our perfect blueprint. Every single person on earth is different. We look different; we talk different. Our shape and attitude are different. We are all unique. So why do we live in a society where a particular body figure is the "right" figure? There is no right body figure. None. Every shape and size is just as perfect as other shapes and sizes.

We create in our minds an illusion of perfection. And we strive for that state of perfection. When we cannot achieve it, because it is imaginary, we become sad and depressed. But in reality we are striving for a perfection that we already obtain. We are the mold of perfection. We are the blueprint of perfection because no other blueprint exists. Every single person has their own blueprint of perfection encoded in them.

So why do we hide our own perfection?

We live in a world of constant competition. We think we need at least as good of a car as the next-door neighbor, as big of a house as our co-worker, and of course the bigger the TV, the more comfort we live in.

Well, do we need any of this stuff to live a better life? The answer is no. We don't need to have as much as the couple next door or your cousin that makes a half million dollars a year. Always remember that happiness does not come from and cannot come from anything that you buy or acquire. Happiness is not really a feeling. Happiness is a state of being. Happiness occurs when all parts of your life are balanced.

CHAPTER 9   **Top things that contribute to stress and a**

We need to learn that it is not important how much m someone else has. It does not matter how good of shape the person down the street is in. It should not matter how big their house is. We need to be content with ourselves. When we start to compare what we have to others, we feel inferior. This inferiority makes the ego want more. The ego makes you believe that when you acquire more, you will receive more happiness. Remember, this is just an illusion.

Constantly comparing yourself to someone else creates stress and anxiety. And keep in mind, when you try to compete against someone else because of what they have, they feel this energy from you when you interact with them. If they are not grounded, their ego will be defensive. Then ego suddenly attacks ego.

You are perfect. You are whole. Only when we start comparing ourselves to other people who we strive to be like, do we think we are imperfect. Not only does Hollywood give the illusion of the perfect body, hair, look, and personality in movies, TV shows, magazines, and media, but also they do it in a very manipulating way, using photo-editing software to enhance their looks and make them look like the common perception of perfection.

If we continue to strive to become a perfection that does not exist, we will inevitably attract stress and anxiety into our lives. How could we not? If we are striving to achieve something that does not exist, we would have to experience stress and this will lead to anxiety. You have to realize that even though perfection, as we think of perfection, is an illusion, you are perfect just the way you are. Everyone is different. Everyone is

77

whole. Everyone is perfect. This does not mean that you should not strive to achieve your physical goals. Striving to be fit is a great goal, as long as it's done for the right reason, to achieve maximum health, and not only to look a certain way.

It is also important to realize that wanting to look attractive or in shape is not always a negative thing. It only becomes negative when this goal becomes more important than being content with our looks. This is when the ego is activated and wants to change practically every part of who we are to look like the models that we see on television.

Always remember that if someone has a problem with the way you look, sound, or act, it is actually their problem and not yours. When someone has a problem with the way you dress, speak, or act, it is just a reflection of how discontent their mind is. If they lived a completely peaceful life, they would not have a problem with you. The second that you take offense to their discontent with you, you automatically make their problem your problem. Then it's ego against ego.

Accepting exactly the way that you are reduces stress and anxiety and boosts self-esteem.

Smile, you are perfect.

Challenge vs. problem

One of the biggest problems people have in their day-to-day lives is their perception of struggle. Most people think their problems are just that, problems. If they are confronted with physical pain, emotional pain, or any kind of family issue, they believe the pain is there to hurt them with no greater benefit. This type of thinking causes so much pain, discomfort, and agony in our everyday lives.

We need to realize the true reason of struggle. We need to start to accept the true reason behind any form of discomfort. It is not to weaken us. It's not to ultimately destroy us. It is actually present to strengthen us so that we can face future struggle more efficiently. Imagine if you have never caught a cold or flu. How would your immune system develop? Imagine if you have never played anyone better than you in sports. How could you get better? Imagine if you never ripped your muscle fibers apart when you work out. How could your muscles grow? It would be impossible.

Struggle is presented in our lives to help us grow and to better equip us to face future struggle more efficiently. But most people curse struggle. Most people hate any form of discontent. When you look at struggle as you are meant to, not only does the situation become so much easier to handle, but also you eventually switch your perception to actually welcome struggle, because you know it's growing and developing your character.

The only way that struggle does not make you grow and develop is when you do not face the struggle naturally. When faced with struggle, so many people try to numb the pain. They drink or mask the pain with recreational drugs. This is robbing nature's opportunity to build resilience within you. The pain is not meant to be numbed. It's meant to be felt so that you learn from it. It's meant to be experienced so that you know not to do that particular thing again. When someone numbs the pain with any form of external substance, the ability to grow and develop character vanishes.

Imagine that we had a device that could cover the sky every time it rained. If we were to do this, vegetation would not grow, livestock would not be able to eat, trees would not grow, and we would not receive clean oxygen or water to drink. Humanity would cease to exist. Rain and snowstorms are a necessary part of nature. In fact, you cannot appreciate the sun without the rain. The same holds true for life. Struggles have to occur in order for us to grow and develop. It's a must.

When we start to look at struggle as an opportunity to grow, we start to walk in the midst of struggle with a smile on our face. If you can do this, you are becoming awakened.

Television

There are billions of bits of information all around us. We can consciously be aware of about 2,000 bits per second. But what about all the bits of information around you that you are not aware of. What about the hundreds of cars and details on each car that you pass on the highway? What about all the sounds and sights in the shopping mall that you are not aware of but you are seeing and hearing? Where does that information go? All of it gets soaked up into your subconscious mind where it is stored forever. This information shapes the way you see the world, what you crave, and what you desire. Everything that you see, hear, taste, touch, and feel is trapped in your subconscious mind and will shape who you are and who you become.

So the question is what are you watching on television? Shows full of drama and violence are affecting your health. It has to. Everything you see and hear is shaping the way you interact with people, your energy level, and how effective your immune system is in healing you.

What kind of shows to avoid:

- Soap operas.

- The evening news. (It likes to concentrate on the negative news.)

- Shows or movies that emphasize violence.

- Shows or movies that emphasize sex.

- Shows that disturb the viewer.

All these shows are changing your brain chemistry. Remember, it is usually not one big thing that causes stress and anxiety. But the dozens of little things we do on a regular basis is actually creating the stress, anxiety, and depression.

When you watch a show exhibiting negative behavior, such as a murder, your brain interprets what you are seeing as reality. Even though your conscious mind knows it is just a scene on a television show, your subconscious mind interprets it as if it is happening right in front of you.

If you were to see a murder in reality your mind and body would react according to your sensitivity to the act. You would tense up, your heart would beat fast, you would sweat, your breathing would become very shallow and you would start to release the stress hormone, cortisol, throughout your body. So even though you are watching a movie and witness a murder your subconscious mind believes that this is taking place in reality. Your body and mind will not react as intensely as it would if you were watching a real murder in front of you but it will react to some degree. Sometimes this reaction is unnoticed but rest assured the body and mind are still reacting.

The more and more you watch negative TV shows or movies you continue to react negatively to some degree. Over time this will do more damage on your health than you can ever imagine.

Video games

When my brother and I were growing up, the most violence we had on video games were Mario and Luigi jumping over turtles heads. Nowadays the amount of realistic violence in video games is unbelievable. The blood, gore, screams, moans, and groans are so realistic that you would think you're actually in the presence of someone being murdered. All these images are being trapped into the back of the viewer's mind. I am not suggesting these types of video games are going to influ child to pick up a gun and go shoot someone, but these games are weakening their immune system.

Just imagine that you are walking down the street and you see two people fighting. You see blood flying and you feel the agony of the person being kicked in the face while he is on the ground. How do you feel? Of course, you are not going to feel joy or happiness because you can relate to what it feels like to be hurt. You are probably going to feel stress, anxiety, anger, and fear. Well, when someone is playing a video game that is displaying the same type of behavior, the brain interprets the behavior as if it's actually happening in front of them. And although you know that you are only playing a video game and it is not actually happening in reality, the brain does not know the difference. Remember, the brain does not interpret the difference between something that is actually happening and when you have a thought of that thing happening. When you think about something that triggers stress, the brain thinks that is actually happening. These thoughts trigger the release of all the chemicals that cause you to experience stress.

So even though when you are playing a violent video game, it is not as severe as watching an actual fight break out, your subconscious mind is recording and reacting to all of the violence, and is triggering the release of cortisol (the stress hormone) from the adrenal gland even on a minuscule level.

Remember, it is hardly ever the one big, traumatic experience causing you prolonged anxiety. It is the dozens of little things that you do on a regular basis causing you to experience anxiety.

Violent video games may not ever influence someone to pick up a knife and go stab someone, but regular exposure to violence through the medium of video games will absolutely affect the wellbeing of each and every one of the people that play them.

Avoid them at all costs.

Music

Most people today listen to music. There are all kinds of genres of music. And there are many kinds of music that calm the body, help relax thoughts, and soothe the soul. But most of the music that you listen to on the top forty week by week is actually affecting you in ways that you are most likely completely oblivious to.

Remember, the subconscious mind can register and record about 400 billion bits of information per second. Everything you see, taste, touch, smell, or hear is being recorded by the subconscious mind. And it's crucial to repeat that the brain does not know the difference between something that is happening and the thoughts about the same thing happening. So when you are listening to music, you are obviously hearing lyrics. When you are listening to music, you are recording every single beat, instrument, and lyric into your subconscious mind, whether or not you are aware of what you are listening to. If the lyrics are saying, "My girlfriend cheated on me," or "My heart is breaking," your brain thinks this is actually happening in your reality. And your brain reacts as if the statement were actually true. Remember the placebo effect? In the placebo effect, the illness that the person is going through is cured from the belief that the sugar pill, which they believe to be a pharmaceutical drug, is going to cure them. Because their brain believed this, belief changed their physiology.

Imagine if you just found out your best friend's boyfriend is cheating on her. How would you feel? You would feel anger, hatred, hurt, stress, and probably even vengeance. Remember, all these emotions are not because of what happened. It's because of your psychological reaction to what happened. Everyone has a built up association of what it's like to be cheated on, whether or not they have experienced it themselves. When you hear that your best friend is being cheated on, your brain reacts and triggers the release of all the chemicals that make you feel stress, anxiety, hatred, etc.

When you are cheated on, the amount of discomfort is at 100%. When your friend is cheated on, the discomfort rate is probably at about 60%. When you hear a stranger is being cheated on, although you don't know this person, you know the pain they are going through. Your discomfort level is at about 20%. So keep in mind that when you hear lyrics in songs, such stories about being cheated on, your brain still reacts on some capacity. You may not feel it in the moment, but your brain reacts to "cheating" and thinking that the event is actually taking place. So even though you may be reacting at only a 5% level of discomfort, you are still reacting! So the more you listen to these types of songs, the more your brain reacts. One song of this nature may pump you up at first, but if you continue to listen to it over and over again, or any type of song with negative lyrics, your brain reacts as if what you are listening to is actually happening. And although you do not realize this, it is actually affecting your health and wellbeing. Most people don't notice this because they are immersed in it. The only way to truly feel how much negative songs affect you is by not listening to them for several months. And then try to listen to them again and see how it feels. You will most definitely notice a huge difference in the level of joy that you experience.

Whatever lyrics you listen to in songs are being recorded into your subconscious mind and will have an impact on you, whether or not you are aware of this. In the moment, you may feel like the music is pumping you up and motivating you, but don't be tricked into temporary feelings of satisfaction. This temporary feeling of satisfaction is like eating a huge chocolate cake by yourself. It may feel good in the moment, but it will always have repercussions. As we talked about earlier, alcohol has the same temporary feeling of satisfaction. It may feel good in the moment but always has repercussions in the end.

There is definitely something to be said in terms of music having a positive effect on the body and mind. There are tons of songs that calm the body and even stimulate in a great way. Choose wisely. It may be in your best interest to filter what you and your kids listen to. Although it does not sound like a big deal, what goes into your ears will always affect you, whether or not you are aware of this.

The subconscious mind records everything. Period. Remember, you are always a reflection of what you are listening to. The people with stressful thoughts are typically the people who are attracted to lyrics of a negative nature. If you are one of those people attracted to this type of music, it's time to sit back and ask yourself, "why?" Then take action.

Friends

I once heard a statement that you are the result of your three closest friends. There is a lot of truth in this statement. Once again, we are always a reflection of whom we attract into our lives. Who wants to hang around people who gossip? Obviously, other people that gossip want to hang around people that gossip. Who wants to hang around people that are constantly trying to find the negative in every situation? Other pessimists want to be around these types of people. Who wants to hang around people who really take care of their bodies every day? Other people who exercise every day gravitate towards these people. It is not a huge scientific discovery that people who have a particular personality, interests, behaviors, and way of life always are attracted to the people who have a similar personality, interests, behaviors, and way of life. The odd part is that a lot of the time people question why their friends are treating them a certain way. When in fact, the same types of personalities and people are being attracted to the person who is wondering why their friends are the way they are.

We always attract whom we are most like. Let's say for example that you love to gossip and you love to go for walks every day. You and your best friend go for a walk every day and you talk up a storm about your co-worker's boyfriend who is supposedly cheating. Or maybe you just heard that your next-door neighbor, who has a wife of ten years, is now seeing his secretary on the side. Since your walks are comprised of story after story of this juicy gossip, your walks typically fly by because of the stories that you are exchanging. So let's say you turn a new leaf and decide to stop gossiping. You meet your friend the next day for your daily 5:00 p.m. walk. Your friend greets you with a smile and starts up the gossip train all over again, as expected, like every other day. But this time you don't feed into it. She tells you about the guy that just moved in down the street. He is flirting with her next-door neighbor that is pregnant by her husband. You don't give in to the gossip train and change the subject, mentioning how beautiful the day is. Your friend agrees and dives right back into the juicy news. You once again, change the subject and talk about a new cooking class that you just signed up for. Your friend shows genuine interest in your new hobby, but goes right back to the story that she started the walk with. Once again, you change the subject by telling her about your newly found interest in cooking. Your friend may try to change the subject by bringing up another juicy story, but you continue to change the subject by bringing up something of a completely different non-gossiping nature. Eventually, what will happen? Because gossiping was a pivotal part of the walk for so many years, it will seem to your friend like the connection between the two of you is somewhat lost. She will eventually start to want to walk less and less with you because it simply isn't the same anymore. What is actually happening is that because you changed, the people that were previously attracted to you will start to be less attracted to you.

CHAPTER 9   **Top things that contribute to stress and anxiety.**

Let's look at the situation from another perspective. Let's say that you took great care of your body, were optimistic, and your hobbies were cooking, playing sports, and volunteering. You met someone that shared the same enthusiasm for these things, the two of you fell in love, and spend most of your time together doing what you both value so much. Then all of a sudden, you started to change. You begin to hang out in nightclubs, you pick up drinking, and you decide to experiment with recreational drugs. Do you think your girlfriend would stick around during this change? She would lose every connection that she has built with you. Because you have changed, she will be repelled because you are not like her anymore.

We always attract exactly whom we are most like. This does not mean that we have to have the same exact hobbies or like the same sports. I am talking about a deeper, more profound type of attraction. I am talking about core fundamental values. Core fundamental values may include taking care of your physical body, honesty, modesty, faith, optimism, openness, etc. So although friends or partners may show differences in the different ways that these core values are exhibited, they tend to have the same core values.

The next time you question why a friend or partner is constantly mistreating you, ask yourself why you are attracted to this person in the first place. You will eventually start to realize that you are attracted to this person because you on some level are this person. People tend to stick around in abusive relationships (friends or intimate relationships), because they have a low self-esteem. A low self-esteem is the result of their negative thoughts about themselves. Remember,

89

thoughts control us. Obviously, someone who chooses to abuse another person, physically, verbally, or emotionally, is holding that same type of negative energy as the person being abused. Someone who truly loved themselves would not stick around in an abusive relationship. They would get up and leave because they value the greatest gift they were ever given, their life.

We need to learn that it is completely okay to sometimes step away from our friends. If friends are dragging you down, constantly trying to fill your world full of gossip and negative news, it is completely okay to not spend as much time with them. You will notice the more you try to take care of your life, the more you will be repelled by negative people. Like always attracts like. You will not have to put in an effort of wanting to be less attracted to negative people once you start to live a more positive life. It will automatically happen. If you were living a negative lifestyle, drinking, going out to clubs, doing recreational drugs, constantly gossiping, eating nothing but unhealthy food, and then changed your life completely around, who would you start being attracted to? You would start to be attracted to people who are like you. So when you wonder why you continue to attract bad situations and negative people into your life, it is time to change you.

Before wishing for the people around you to change, try changing yourself first, and see what happens. It's okay to leave friends if they are committed to dragging you down. Believe me when I say, if you are living a negative life and start to clean up your life, your negative friends will not want to hang out with you anyway. It will be a transition because you will miss the company of your previous friends. This will fade away as new people will be attracted into your life and you will start to be attracted to the people who are on your same frequency.

Sometimes the negative people in your life are family members or even your kids. Then there is an issue of not being in a position to disassociate from them. But that's okay. This does not mean you have to completely stop being in contact with them. It simply means that you don't have to hang out with them or talk to them as much.

It's their problem, not yours

If you feel like you have to impress your friends, boyfriend, girlfriend, etc. with brand name clothes, designer shoes, or impressive skills, you don't. Feeling this desire comes from your ego. Your ego believes the people that you need to attract into your life are the people that care about these superficial things. And rest assured, every single time you satisfy your ego's materialistic craving, you are growing a deeper, darker sense of craving the material world.

The people that truly care about you; care about "you." Not what you wear, how you talk, or your social status. Do you think your dog cares about what you wear? Do you think your dog cares about what kind of car your buying next or how long your hair is? Do you think your baby is embarrassed to sit next to you because there is dirt on your shirt?

When you sit down and think about it, if you're the type of person that is allowing stress to appear in your life because of what others will think of you, you are allowing your peace to be robbed by giving this ability to other people. The reality is, the people that truly care about you are the people that couldn't care less what you wear, how much money you make, or what you look like. They love and appreciate you, for you.

If you are attracting superficial people into your life, it's because you put too much value on superficial things. We only attract what we are most like. Obviously, we live in a world where we have to dress appropriate as our jobs may depend on it, we should talk properly if we are meeting someone for the first time, and we should be mannerly in practically all situations. But the problem occurs when we start to compare ourselves with others and it takes over our lives, causing unneeded stress.

You have the ability to stop comparing. You have the ability to live a life completely independent of what others have. You have the ability to sit next to your friends, showing off the clothes that you can afford, not the clothes that put you in debt just because it's a brand name. You have the ability to realize the people that truly care about you are the people that truly don't care about the superficial things in your life.

You are completely whole. You are absolutely the way you should be. You don't need anything external to create happiness. Nothing that you can buy can create peace. By simply altering your mind and calming your ego, you will find a peace that already exists within you.

Change yourself, see the universe unfold, and attract exactly who you are most like in your life.

CHAPTER 9   **Top things that contribute to stress and anxiety.**

Toxic thoughts

Imagine that you awoke one morning, stretched and complained about the thought of facing the cold outside on a brisk January day. But all of a sudden, a smile came over your face because today you would wear your brand new $80 brand name hoodie that your father bought for you the day before. It instantaneously brought your sadness level from a ten down to a nine. You get out of bed and rush to the bathroom to see if the pimple on your forehead shrunk during your stressful eight-hour sleep. It didn't. Don't worry; you have concealer that always comes in handy in times like these. You dab it on, and like magic, the pimple disappears. Sadness level is down to an eight. You get ready to eat breakfast but notice that your belly is not quite as hard as you'd like it to be to win over your junior high crush. So, you skip breakfast in hopes that it will shrink just a little more. The sadness factor slips down to seven.

You walk down the street just as the bus is pulling up and jump on board. Seeing that you are one of the last stops, all the seats are just about filled but one. It's by one of the unpopular kids that are not wearing brand name clothing. In fact, you can tell the clothing is secondhand. You don't have a choice but to sit with him. Your anxiety level increases as you don't want your crush to see you sit with one of the un-cool kids. Just as you're about to sit down, you hear one of your friends shout your name, and notice in the corner of your eye an empty seat next to him. You make a dash for the back of the bus and sit down beside him. Your sadness level drops to a six.

Jeremy Bennett

You arrive at the school and are greeted by one of the cool kids in front of your crush. Your sadness level drops two levels instantaneously. You're down to a four! You pack your books in your locker when you realize you have a physical education class and you get to show off your brand new designer track pants. Down to three!

You confidently walk to the gym with your chin held high as you are showing off your brand new running shoes. Down to two. You enter the gym and line up against the wall as two captains are chosen to pick teams. It's the first captain's pick. It's you!

The sadness level drops down to one! You feel joy!

The game starts and you're doing fantastic. Your energy level is through the roof and no one around you can keep up. You score multiple goals and the physical education teacher pats you on the back for a game well played. You go to the dressing room with your head held high and look in the mirror with a huge bright smile on your face, until you notice the sweat from your forehead washed away the concealer that was masking your pimple. All you can see is the huge red pimple sticking out of your head. You panic and frantically search through your gym bag only to realize that you left your concealer makeup at home! You're anxiety level shoots through the roof as you know your crush is going to see the huge pimple within minutes. You don't know what to do, so you crawl into one of the stalls and wait for all your classmates to leave the dressing room. Then no one will see the catastrophe growing out of your head. The coast is clear and you tiptoe out of the dressing room and return to your locker, grab your cell phone, and call your mother, telling her that you're not feeling well and for her to come pick you up.

You return home, crawl in bed, and shake with fear that you almost experienced a nightmare. Oh, and you're back to ten.

Researchers are telling us we have up to 60,000 thoughts every single day. Read that again and think about how active our minds are. Thinking 60,000 thoughts every single day is a sure way to burn out. The human brain is not meant to think these amounts of thoughts every single day. I once heard, "The mind should be used like a tool. You pick up the tool when you need to use it, and put it back down after finishing." But most people do the complete opposite. In fact, they think that they are being unproductive if they are not thinking. Yes, we obviously have to use our minds to think. Without the ability to think, we would be animal-like.

But here is the sad news. Not only are most people thinking up to 60,000 thoughts every single day, but also most of these thoughts are the same thoughts they had yesterday. It doesn't stop there. Not only are the large majority of these thoughts the same as yesterday, they are negative thoughts, either dwelling on something negative that happened in the past or fearing something that could potentially happen in the future.

Remember, the brain does not know the difference between something that is actually happening and when you think about something happening. The brain thinks that whatever you are thinking about right now is actually taking place right now. Then it releases chemicals into your blood that make you feel stressed out, which could lead to anxiety or in many cases an anxiety attack.

Right now, think about something in your past that really triggers a lot of stress in you. Maybe someone cheated on you; you lost your job, or maybe you had a physical altercation with a prior friend. Really, try to see yourself back then and you will notice that your mood will shift. You will start to lose energy. Your hands may become a little sweaty and you may even experience some anxiety. If the event you are thinking about is traumatic enough, there is the possibility that you may even have an anxiety attack. But how could you have an anxiety attack from something that has already taken place and is not taking place right now? It is because your brain thinks that it is happening right now. The brain does not understand past or future. It works in accordance to right now. So, when you think about the past, your brain thinks that whatever you are thinking about is taking place right now. That's why you feel stress or uneasiness. The same holds true for thinking about the future. If you think about something negative that could happen in the future, your brain interprets those thoughts as happening right now. That's why you react with fear, uneasiness, or anxiety.

So consider your, on average, 60,000 thoughts a day. If these are typically thoughts about something bad from the past or something that you fear may happen, this is dramatically affecting your health and wellbeing. You are not only stressing yourself out, but you are losing energy, elevating your blood pressure, and weakening your immune system, all from thoughts that you have every single day.

CHAPTER 9   Top things that contribute to stress and anxiety.

Every single negative thought triggers the release of cortisol (the stress hormone) into your bloodstream. Remember, it's your thoughts about situations, not the situations themselves that release this hormone. Your thoughts control everything. It creates you to be exactly who you are. So yes, we need to think. It's what distinguishes us from the animal kingdom. But for the most part we use the beautiful gift of our minds against us. We use it to think about the things that went wrong in the past or to think about what could possibly go wrong tomorrow, next week, or next year. This is abusing one of the most special gifts we have ever been blessed with, the mind.

Let's look at how depression is usually created. Let's say you are in great health and you typically do the things on a daily basis that contributes to a healthy lifestyle. You are outside playing soccer with your kids when your husband walks up to you and says, "Lisa, from down the street was just in a serious car accident. The ambulance just rushed her to the hospital." You suddenly lose all your energy and your level of enthusiasm decreases dramatically. Lisa is your kids' babysitter. Even though you are not close with Lisa and only hired her a time or two to babysit your children, you feel sadness every time you think of what happened.

So you go into the house because you lost all energy to play soccer with your children. You sit on the couch and your mind starts to race about how serious the accident really was. You think more and more and soon realize that it is draining every bit of energy out of you. You know you need to take your mind off of it, so you preoccupy your mind with your hobby, tying salmon flies. After an hour of this, your mind seems at ease and you regain your energy level back.

So what is my point? My point is that your thoughts of the news of Lisa getting into a car accident drained all your energy. You didn't want to be active anymore and wanted to just go relax on the couch. Imagine if you thought about this every single hour, or every single minute. How would your body feel? Your body would feel drastically drained. You wouldn't have energy to do anything.

Think about anything that triggers stress in you and notice how this drains you. One negative thought can drain you of all your energy. Keep in mind that researchers are telling us we have, on average, 60,000 thoughts a day. Think about a person who constantly is thinking negative thoughts and how draining that must be. If someone continues to think negative thoughts, the body is going to be accustomed to this new type of energy level, which is practically no energy at all. When this happens day after day, week after week, and month after month, the body and mind goes into a depression state. The person no longer has any energy to do what they normally used to love doing, and not wanting to get out of bed becomes their predominate state. The person then becomes clinically depressed.

Thoughts control who we are and what we become. If we could learn to control our thoughts, switch our negative thoughts to positive thoughts, and switch our typical lifestyle of being controlled by the ego to living a state of being predominately in the present moment, stress would cease to exist. Anxiety would be a thing of the past, and depression would never be experienced.

Later in the book, I will show you exactly what you need to do to break out of this habit. Applying this one lesson alone can completely transform your life, rid you of stress, and ultimately take away all of your needless anxiety.

Social environments

Where do you like to hang out in your spare time? Is it around family, playing board games, sporting events, the local fitness facility? Or is it in toxic environments like clubs, house parties, or other social events where alcohol/drugs are a factor. Remember, a very easy way to find out how psychologically healthy you are is to simply ask yourself what you like to do in your spare time. Where do you like to go on the weekends? If we are attracted to toxic environments like clubs, this always means that we are having toxic thoughts. We are attracted to whatever we are most like.

Clubs, in particular, are one of the worst places that you could possibly hang out in. Who is attracted to clubs? People who want, crave, and desire alcohol (for the most part) hang out and are attracted to the club scene. Who craves alcohol? People who want to numb their mind, due to toxic thoughts, crave alcohol. You will notice that the more toxic the thoughts are, the more they want to drink. Drinking alcohol has nothing to do with morality, good or bad, ethical or unethical. Wanting to numb the mind with a toxic substance simply means there is a reason for wanting to numb the mind. You want to numb it when you don't like the thoughts in your mind. If your thoughts were peaceful, optimistic, and loving, you would not have any desire to numb it with a toxic substance. Why would you?

Most club goers think that it's completely fine to hang out in the clubs scenes. They may say, "I am not causing any trouble" or "I am not hurting anyone" or "I am just hanging out with my friends." But we really need to analyze why someone is attracted to what they are attracted to. Our thoughts call the shots. Our thoughts are the pilot in our lives. Whatever thoughts we hold, we create in our reality. If you are constantly thinking about eating a scrumptious chocolate cake all day long and then suddenly you walk past a store displaying a chocolate cake in the window, you are going to be attracted to it that much more. But if you weren't thinking about eating that chocolate cake all day, chances are you would walk by the cake and barely even notice it.

The same holds true for negative thoughts. The more negative thoughts we have, the more negative places and situations that we are attracted to. Whatever we think most, we are attracted to most. If you still don't believe this, think about what happens when you buy a new car. You start to see that car everywhere. You see it on the highway, in parking lots; you start to notice several people in your neighborhood own the same car. But ask yourself, why did you not notice these cars before you bought your car. You did not notice them because you did not own one yourself. If you did not own one yourself, you were not thinking about it as if you would when you just bought the car. You will also realize that once the newness wears off your new car and you start to get bored of it, you will not notice the other cars half as much.

CHAPTER 9   **Top things that contribute to stress and anxiety.**

Whatever preoccupies our mind on a daily basis is what we are attracted to most and what catches our attention most. Need another example? What happens when you buy a new TV? The next time you go into a stranger's house, you are drawn to their TV. You look for the brand name to see if it's the same as yours. You mentally calculate the dimensions in your head and analyze the resolution. Or what happens when you buy a new pair of running shoes and you go to the gym the next day? You start to notice all the other people in the gym wearing the same running shoes as yours. Why didn't you recognize that they were wearing those running shoes the day before you bought yours? It is because you did not own a pair yourself. And if you did not own the same pair, obviously, you would not be thinking about that particular pair of shoes. We are attracted to what we think about most. Always.

When you enter a club, you have to realize that most of the people are there to numb their minds. If they are there to numb their mind, this is obviously a reflection of how toxic their thoughts are, whether they know it or not. Some club goers will argue this and say they are happy people, completely content with their lives and psychological health. But keep in mind that "life" is what we experience when we are not intoxicated. So if someone is craving a substance that will intoxicate them and numb their minds, then they are obviously not content and satisfied with their life. That is why they want to numb their minds.

When being in the midst of hundreds of other people in a club, most people have one thing in common; they are all going to numb their minds. If they are all going to numb their minds, they have another thing in common; they are all experiencing overwhelming toxic thoughts. If you are in the presence of hundreds of other people who are in the same boat as you, experiencing overwhelming toxic thoughts, then what situations, relationships, and circumstances are going to arise out of the interactions with the other people there? Toxic environments produce toxic situations.

When you meet someone that is intoxicated, you may fall in love with the false self. Because what they are projecting is a numbed mind, void of all the negative thoughts that normally occupy their mind. Then once you get to know the person, things typically change and their true self starts to show.

Simply put, clubs are one of the very worst places you can hang out if you want to live a healthy life.

Taking life too seriously

The Rain Forest

Imagine that you lived alone on a warm tropical island. The only food that you ate was food that you found or hunted. You didn't have parents, siblings, or friends to entertain you. The only companionship you had was your dog, Lucky. You spent your days walking the island looking for food to eat, which was plentiful. You were never in any immediate danger and the weather was typically sunny with the occasional rainfall, which you welcomed as it filled up your containers with crystal clear drinking water.

CHAPTER 9   Top things that contribute to stress and anxiety.

Close your eyes and imagine this was actually how you lived your life. Think about waking up at 5:00 a.m. to the sunset, the warm air breezing through your hair as you walk out onto the beach to sink your feet in the sand. You get ready to start your day by searching for some fruit. You know the process won't take long, as the island is covered in healthy, nutritious food.

Do you think that you would spend any time at all thinking about how presentable you look for the animals you come across? Do you think your dog Lucky woke up in the morning and expected you to act a certain way, presenting yourself appropriately, cleanly shaved or hair down with curls? When you walked through the forest, do you think you would really care what kind of t-shirt you were wearing or whether you had designer running shoes on? Would it cross your mind to not step out of your house before coating your eyelids with eyeliner or face with blush?

Imagine having to dress up for the animals on the island every day. Imagine stressing yourself out because you're not sure if they are going to like the dress you are wearing or the earrings that hung from your ears. Imagine sitting down in front of a mirror and at 6:00 a.m. asking yourself if you think the monkeys you will see on your walk around the island would prefer your hair up or down. This sounds ludicrous, right?

So, back to reality: Why do we wake up in the morning concerned about how we are going to look, smell, and present ourselves? Why do we care if we are a little overweight and can't fit into our wedding dress? Why do we care if ours arms aren't as defined as the fitness gurus we see on the infomercials? It's because we are in a constant state of comparison. We always want to look as good as the girl down the street or as fit as the guy that our ex-girlfriend is dating. We want to be as smart as the kid next door or as pretty as the Hollywood stars.

We are in a constant battle of inner conflict with ourselves. This conflict is created because we are always trying to compare ourselves to something that does not even exist. It's called perfection. I should say, the illusion of perfection.

It seems that some people who enter our lives simply do not know how to smile. It's like it's their mission to take everything and everyone seriously, like joking is a sin. One of the biggest mistakes we make as humans is feeling the peace and sense of wonderment of a child is wrong because it's simply not adult-like or mature. When was the last time you saw a baby stressed out? You didn't, because babies do not allow their minds to get the best of them. Babies are so present. Whatever they are doing, they are doing. When they are involved in a task, they are not thinking about yesterday and certainly not thinking about tomorrow. The next time you look at a baby doing anything, playing with a toy, watching a cartoon, or blowing bubbles, look at the babies eyes, look at their focus. It is so obvious how in the moment they really are.

Adults tend to lose the wonderment of everyday things. Once, I was doing work on my computer in a local coffee shop when a toddler and his mother walked in front of me. The child wanted to hold his mother's keys. The mother gave the child her keys and it was like that child had discovered some amazing treasure. He was full of excitement and wonder. Adults have

CHAPTER 9   **Top things that contribute to stress and anxiety.**

lost the feeling of what it's like to be a child. We have no idea how much we can learn from children.

When a child wants to laugh, he laughs. When a child wants to cry, he cries. But one thing you will notice about children is that they don't hang on to emotions. They feel them, they experience them, and then they let them go and they become present again. Typical adults hold on to their emotions and allow the emotions to affect their day. They believe that they have to be aware of all the war, negativity, and chaotic events going on around them. And to some extent, it is important to know about our world matters. But when we are not in a position to contribute to helping in some way, then what is the real benefit in knowing every chaotic event that is unfolding? In other words, avoid watching the evening news. The huge majority of the evening news concentrates on the negative news. Oh, and if you are attracted to watching the evening news, it's time to ask yourself why? The answer always lies within your thoughts. If your thoughts are predominately negative then you will be attracted to negativity. The more peaceful your mind is; you will notice that you will no longer be attracted to the evening news.

We need to learn to smile and laugh more. Research has shown us that a smile triggers the release of endorphins (the good feeling chemical) from our brain. Endorphins are neurotransmitters, chemicals that pass along signals from one neuron to the next. Some of the effects of endorphin release are:

- They enhance your mood.

- They reduce stress.

- They reduce anxiety.

- They reduce depression.

- They boost self-esteem.

- They improve sleep.

- And the list goes on and on.

Laughing is shown to release even more endorphins than smiling. Have you ever been involved in a conversation with a friend about something that happened years ago? It was so funny and you started laughing so much that you had pains in your stomach. Did you ever get to a point where you were laughing so much that your mouth was open but no sound was coming out? Try to experience that as much as you can every single day. Laughing heals for several reasons. If you're laughing, you are not stressed. If you are laughing, you are obviously not thinking negative thoughts. If you are laughing, you are releasing endorphins, which have all the benefits listed above.

We need to take life a little less seriously. We need to take time every single day to laugh, smile, and be goofy. We need to make fun of ourselves. Laughing is as simple as watching something funny on our computers or turning on a funny movie. It's as simple as drifting our thoughts back to a time when life seemed easier and life was less serious.

CHAPTER 9   Top things that contribute to stress and anxiety.

Eating toxic food

It's probably no surprise to you that the food most people consume nowadays doesn't even remotely resemble the kind and type of food that mankind ate throughout history. Most people do not eat food anymore. They eat "food-like" products, chemically made in a laboratory in mass quantities. This is not real food! The food is created in laboratories, sold, and marketed as real food. When, in fact, there is nothing real about it.

Food industries process food so it can be stored longer and to make it more appealing. These types of food should not be eaten on a regular basis, and in a perfect world, not at all. Potato chips, candy bars, etc., are heavily processed, providing practically no nutritional benefit to the body.

One important fact we have to realize is that food is meant to bring the body nourishment, energy, and fuel to live a productive day. Nowadays, the food most people put into their bodies is destroying practically every organ that makes up their body. Chemical after chemical, artificial sweeteners such as aspartame, high amounts of fat, sugar, salt, MSG, processed meats, and very addictive qualities make this type of food a nightmare for the body.

Life and our bodies are the greatest gift that we have ever received. Why would we want to abuse it? What we put into our bodies is supposed to fuel us, give us energy, and nourish us so that we stay healthy. Imagine buying a new car. You clean and wax it every single day but pour soda into the gasoline tank. Do you think that your car would appreciate this? The car wouldn't even start. You would never do this to your car. Keep in mind that your car is a material object, easily replaceable. But yet we would never do this to our vehicle, because we know if we pour anything other than what we are supposed to into the gasoline tank, the car will not start.

The same holds true for our bodies. We are not meant to eat chemicals. We are not designed to drink alcohol. We are not meant to consume recreational drugs or eat foods high in fat, sugars, or salt. The body does not like this and responds accordingly. Why do you think that after drinking so much alcohol you throw up? Throwing up is a defense mechanism designed by the brain to send a signal to your body that a poisonous substance is in you. And you have to get rid of it as soon as possible, before it does any more harm than it has already done.

When you consume unhealthy food, you feel groggy, un-energetic, and sometimes even depressed. There is a very good reason for this. This is the side effect of trying to fuel your body with the wrong type of fuel. The main reason that we eat should be to effectively fuel our bodies and nourish it with what we need to keep the body healthy. It should not be only to satisfy our taste buds.

It's important to realize why you crave unhealthy food. Remember, everything we crave is a reflection of the thoughts we hold in our mind and our predominant subconscious beliefs. People with low self-esteem tend not to fuel their bodies right, with healthy, organic food. A girl who recently broke up with her boyfriend tends to crave a "comfort" food, such as ice cream, because the tastiness of the ice cream attracts her thoughts to the satisfaction of the taste, thus temporarily taking her mind off her breakup. Remember, anything that you put into your body to "de-stress" you is masking the pain of what is causing you discomfort (your thoughts). A toxic mind will always be attracted to toxic food. If you find yourself eating a lot of junk food, examine your thoughts.

A person who cherishes their life, their body, and their health obviously has less toxic thoughts than someone who does not take care of these things. If you have a peaceful, healthy mind, you will not be attracted to unhealthy food.

Food affects your stress, anxiety, and depression levels by changing your state of mind. If you continue to eat junk food and avoid fresh, organic food, you will most likely gain weight, which usually causes a decrease in your self-esteem. That can make you feel groggy and depressed. When you feel any kind of psychological discomfort, the ego loves to kick in and make your mind think about everything that is wrong in your life. As the old saying goes, misery loves company. This not only applies to attracting negative people into your life, it applies to your negative thoughts attracting negative thoughts. It is a spiral. Once you start to eat bad food, you feel down. When you feel down, your ego takes over and it will throw at you a million other reasons to feel down. You will start to think about the bad day you had last week or the potential bad day you will have tomorrow.

When you go shopping for groceries, stick to the outer extremity of the grocery store. Here you will find the vegetables, fruit, and other fresh food. You will notice that when you start shopping for "food" in the isles, the ingredients labels will be filled with chemicals, toxins, and loads of ingredients that most people have no idea how to pronounce. If you cannot pronounce the ingredient, it is best to stay away from it.

We need to eat food for the one reason that it is designed for; to nourish and energize us so that we can affectively get through our day and accomplish what we have to do while feeling great, with high energy levels and focus.

Overview of what causes anxiety

We have to understand and really grasp that we create our own anxiety and that it is a defense mechanism created by the brain to help us. Without anxiety, we would continue to do the thing that is destroying our bodies and minds. Anxiety is a friend, just like physical pain warns us to take our hand off the hot burner on a stove, anxiety is a warning to say that we are abusing our minds and bodies and we need to stop for it to go away.

We need to give thanks to anxiety and stop hating a friend that is trying to take care of us. The second we experience anxiety, we need to sit back and analyze what we are doing wrong in our lives and then address the cause, not take a pill, hoping it will eventually go away. We need to get to the root of the anxiety and address it. The wonderful thing is that when we get to the root cause of the anxiety and address it, not only does our anxiety go away, but also all areas of our lives improve.

CHAPTER 9 **Top things that contribute to stress and anxiety.**

It has to! When you get to the root cause of what is causing your anxiety, you create resilience, dedication, commitment, and understanding. All these qualities affect every other area of your life.

Needless complaining triggers the release of the stress hormone, cortisol. So does gossiping, judging, or ridiculing anyone. Every time that you plan revenge in your mind or wish harm upon someone, you are holding negative thoughts. These negative thoughts create stress, which just attracts more stress and leads to anxiety.

Drinking alcohol is robbing your ability to build resilience. We are not meant to artificially numb our minds. This is a crutch and will never treat the cause of why you want to de-stress. We need to face our struggles naturally, build immunity and resilience, so that we will be equipped to handle future struggle much more efficiently. The same holds true for using recreational drugs to relax. Keep in mind, when I talk about using recreational drugs to relax, I am not referring to using some substances for medicinal purposes.

Comparing what we don't have to what others have will only make us want to be more materialistic (which attracts stress) and look down upon ourselves. We know that the ego is alive and well when we start to feel that we are not as adequate as the couple down the street. Happiness does not and will not ever come from anything we acquire. Happiness occurs in a person when all areas of their lives are balanced and presence is a predominate state of living. Instead of being jealous of what your co-worker, neighbor, or friend has, be happy for them.

When you can genuinely feel joy for what another person has, then you know that your ego is not running the show.

Everything you are exposed to, your subconscious mind records. What we are exposed to creates subconscious beliefs. And whatever subconscious beliefs we have shapes our physiology, exactly who and what we attract, and our entire reality. In a perfect world, we would only be watching educational shows on television, listening to uplifting music, and if video games had to exist, they would be of an educational nature emphasizing life lessons.

Friends should be in our lives to lift us up, teach us lessons, and be there for us when we need them. They shouldn't be there to pressure us into harming our body by drinking alcohol, doing drugs, or filling our minds full of toxic thoughts. It is totally okay to gently exit the lives of some people when we know that deep down they are not a healthy influence. We need to learn to take care of ourselves before we can help anyone else. When you are in an airplane and the flight attendant is going over the safety procedures, notice what they say. They say that if the plane happens to dispense the oxygen mask to make sure and put the mask on your face before helping anyone else. How could you possibly help anyone else if you are gasping for air? You cannot. You have to take care of yourself first and make sure that you are healthy before you can help anyone else. It's okay to make new friends and leave negative friends behind. Of course, if they need your help or they need a shoulder to cry on, help them. But this does not mean you have to be in their presence as much as you used to be. This is draining and feeding into their ego because they know if you are there to entertain their negative lifestyle, then they will continue to live that particular lifestyle.

We have on average 60,000 thoughts a day. We shouldn't. Resting the mind is one of the greatest things we can do to get rid of stress, anxiety, and depression. Hanging out in nightclubs will only attract negative situations and people in your lives as the people that go there do it to numb their minds. If they are numbing their minds, they are numbing it because of toxic thoughts. Being in the presence of hundreds of toxic minds can only result in toxic situations. Avoid toxic environments!

Avoid junk food. Eat foods that have one ingredient. Laugh. Smile. Learn to be goofy. Never lose the sense of childhood. It heals more than you can ever imagine. Learn to look at life's struggles as what they truly are, opportunities to grow and develop into exactly who you can and are meant to be. You know that you are truly starting to become awakened when you look at discomforting situations as opportunities and welcome them with a smile, because you know that once you face it naturally and get through it, you are better equipped to face future struggle more effectively.

Getting through struggle the way we are meant to get through struggle builds character, immunity, and resilience.

Chapter 10

Top things to do to reduce stress and anxiety.

Before getting into this section of the book let's explore a very important question. Nowadays it is fairly easy to figure out how physically healthy we are. We book an appointment with our family physician, they do a physical, send us for some blood work, and a few days later, we know how we are doing. What about how our mental health is doing? How can we analyze how psychologically healthy we are and how can we analyze if and how much our ego is controlling our minds?

We can do this by asking ourselves two simple questions:

Question #1

What do I like to do in my spare time? Ask yourself what are you attracted to on the weekends. Are you attracted to toxic behavior and toxic environments? Are you attracted to drinking, drugs, and negative environments such as nightclubs? Do you crave hanging out with pessimistic people? If you do, this simply means that your ego is getting the best of you and occupying your mind more than it should. A toxic mind (thoughts) is attracted to toxic situations. In the same respect a peaceful mind, where ego is not in control, is attracted to more peaceful situations and people. A peaceful mind is attracted to non-toxic situations, people, and behaviors. It would not be attracted to alcohol because there is no need to numb the mind, as it is peaceful already. It is not attracted to nightclubs, because the people that typically go to nightclubs are trying to numb their mind, as they are not experiencing peaceful thoughts most of the time.

A very toxic mind will be constantly attracted to toxic environments, whereas, a less toxic mind, but still toxic, will be less attracted to toxic environments. A very peaceful mind will never be attracted to toxic environments. Take, for example, a person in fairly good psychological health, who avoids drinking, toxic behaviors, etc., all of a sudden finds out that his wife, for the past two years has been having an affair. He is shocked, saddened, and slips into a state of depression. These depressed thoughts then get the best of him and he slips into trying to numb the pain with alcohol, developing a drinking dependency. In my industry, I see this time and time again.

A toxic mind is attracted to toxic situations. A peaceful mind is attracted to peaceful situations. So ask yourself. What am I attracted to? It will always be a reflection of what state of mind you are in.

Question #2

Ask yourself how long you can sit in a quiet room without any distractions. Someone who has a very peaceful mind and has a mind that is not occupied with toxic thoughts will be able to do this very easily and enjoy the time. But someone who has a mind that is typically full of negative and toxic thoughts tends to need distractions. These distractions help ease the mind by concentrating on the stimulating sound, etc.

Are you the type of person that has to have the radio on, the TV on in the background, or has to be constantly stimulated? Ask yourself why.

Presence

The mind is like a muscle. Imagine trying to bench press 100 pounds ten times. You lift it five times and barely get the sixth one up. You put the bar down and take a thirty-second rest, because you know that all you need is thirty seconds to reenergize and accomplish your task.

Well, the mind needs rest too. It is not meant to be working (thinking) all day. If you are constantly thinking, that means you will eventually burn out. By giving your mind the rest it needs, you rejuvenate it, reenergize it, and release endorphins, the "good-feeling" chemical that defeats stress and anxiety.

Most people have heard of the benefits of meditation and they know it reduces stress, anxiety, and depression. But the reality is that most people don't do it. There is nothing really mysterious about meditation. You don't have to sit in the lotus position with your palms facing the stars to meditate.

CHAPTER 10   **Top things to do to reduce stress and anxiety.**

Meditation simply means that you are focusing on what is going on right now. Not two seconds ago or what's going to happen five seconds from now, but right now. This very moment. The whole purpose of meditation is to calm the mind. When I refer to the mind in this context, I am referring to the thoughts that the mind produces.

Stress and anxiety is caused from an overactive, negative-thinking mind producing hundreds and thousands of negative thoughts. It's important for me to keep emphasizing that situations do not cause stress or anxiety. This is one of the biggest misunderstandings. A situation never causes stress or anxiety; our psychological reaction to the situation causes the stress or anxiety.

Imagine if you were sitting down watching television in your living room while a humongous black bear slowly creeps in with his mouth open, drooling, and teeth as sharp as razor blades. As soon as you turn around to see the vicious animal, you very quickly realize that you are about to become bear food. Your heart starts to beat out of your chest, you get a huge rush of adrenaline, you become sweaty all over your body, and your body tenses up. In other words, you experience anxiety. But what were to happen if the situation was changed around a little. Let's say the black bear did everything identically. He slowly crept in, was still drooling from his wide-open mouth with razor sharp teeth. But, in this case, you did not realize he was there because you were preoccupied with watching the television. How would you react? You would react as if nothing out of the ordinary was happening. The situation in both cases was identical but you reacted in one case with anxiety and in the other case without it. Why? The first time, you knew the bear was there, so this "knowing" simply means that your thoughts created the anxiety. The second time, because you were not aware of the black bear, your thoughts did not react to the situation or cause anxiety. Thoughts cause anxiety, not situations.

So why is meditation so beneficial? Meditation means that you are not thinking any longer. And if you are not thinking, and thinking is the cause of stress and anxiety, how could stress and anxiety possibly exist? It cannot. Right now, close your eyes and try to hear all the sounds that are around you. Most likely, even if you are in a quiet room reading this, you will start to hear sounds that you didn't realize were present. When you head these sounds, try to listen even more attentively. You will start to hear vehicles outside passing on the street, and maybe you hear the internal fan of your computer a few feet away. When you "notice" that you are hearing a particular sound, you cannot think at the same time. So, if you cannot think at the same time, you are obviously not thinking any kind of negative thought. This is meditation. This is calming your mind.

The next time you are driving to work and find your mind drifting off thinking about all the possible things that could go wrong, simply pay attention to what you are passing by on the street. Look at the people. Look at the street signs. Take notice of the make and model of the car that is ahead of you. When you take notice of something, you cannot think at the same time. And once again, if you are not thinking, you obviously cannot think a negative thought.

CHAPTER 10   **Top things to do to reduce stress and anxiety.**

Pick up anything in your hand and look at it as if it is the first time you have ever set eyes upon it. Look at it and analyze every single inch of it. Note the texture, color, firmness, and weight. Look at it out of curiosity, just like a baby looks at something that it holds the very first time. When you look at something out of curiosity, you cannot think at the same time. If you are not thinking, you are obviously not thinking negative thoughts, therefore, not contributing to the feeling of stress and anxiety.

If you want to experience a more formal way of meditating, go to a quiet room and sit down in a comfortable position. Close your eyes and start to breathe nice and slowly. When you start to feel relaxed, put all of your attention on your feet. You will eventually notice that you feel your feet in some capacity, maybe a little warmth, tingle, or coolness. When you start to feel your feet, guess what that means? It means that you are not thinking anymore, and therefore, resting your mind. When you start to feel your feet, move up to your ankles, and once again try to concentrate all of your focus on your ankles. When you start to feel your ankles on some level, this means you are not thinking. Move up to your legs, knees, thighs, and so on. This takes practice and the mind will want to wander. That's okay. Simply bring your attention back to your body. You cannot become a good hockey player by practicing once. It takes time, patience, and practice.

An overactive mind plays a huge role in insomniacs (people who have trouble sleeping). Most of the times these people do not have a physiological issue; it's a mental issue in the form of over active thinking. Meditation can cure this issue once and for all.

Once again, there are many forms of meditation. Have you ever noticed that you feel so good when you play your favorite instrument? Did you ever notice that two hours of playing your favorite sport seems to relax you, or being in the presence of a cute little baby? Why? It's because for that time you are concentrating on what is going on right now, playing your instrument, playing your favorite sport, or gazing at the baby. These are all forms of meditation.

No matter what, I would still recommend that you do not rely on what I call the "present moment conductors." Present moment conductors are the things you encounter on a day-to-day basis. They cause you to become present. Either it takes you off guard, or it's something you really enjoy doing that takes focus and concentration. Remember, you cannot concentrate on something and think about something else at the same time. It is important to do what I call deliberate meditation. Deliberate meditation is when you calm your mind on purpose through the deliberate act of meditation. You can do this the way I describe above by concentrating on your different body parts until you feel them. Another great way to meditate is to simply concentrate on your breath going in and out. When you start to feel your breath going in and out, you cannot think at the same time. This means that you are resting your mind.

Keep in mind there is a right way to breathe and a wrong way to breathe. We breathe, on average, about 20,000 times a day. Guess what, most people breathe incorrectly by breathing shallowly. Receiving more oxygen means we are healing and it can even help reduce chronic pain, atrial fibrillation, asthma, digestive issues, depression, and of course stress and anxiety.

CHAPTER 10   Top things to do to reduce stress and anxiety.

How should you breathe? You have to learn how to breathe with your diaphragm, just like babies. When babies enter this world, they breathe with their diaphragm, not with their chest. Look at a baby when the baby breathes. You'll notice his belly rises when he breathes in and sinks when he breathes out. Not his chest. But as babies become adolescents, teenagers, and then adults, they become lazier and start to breathe the improper way, with their chest. This is limiting the amount of oxygen that is entering the body, and therefore, not allowing the body to receive the amount of oxygen it needs for optimum health.

The typical adult takes about fifteen to twenty breaths per minute, which is three to four times as much as we should be taking. When we continue to breathe shallow breaths, a number of health side effects can occur, like increased stress and anxiety. When you are stressed, one of the first things to happen is that you start to breathe shallowly. This is getting you ready for the flight or fight response. If you have trained your body to breathe on a regular basis in a shallow way, guess what message you are sending to your adrenal gland? You are sending the message that you are stressed out, even if you are not at the time. When you breathe shallowly, you trigger the release of cortisol from the adrenal gland. Our immune system's job is to keep us healthy and fight off the toxins, diseased cells, and bacteria, but when the mind is holding negative thoughts, or you're breathing shallowly, cortisol levels are elevated and the immune cells slow down drastically. Then pathogens and diseased cells have a chance to do damage.

When you take slow, deep breaths and breathe the way we are meant to breathe, with the diaphragm, you automatically boost your immune system, reduce cortisol levels, and take control. The next time you are feeling stressed, concentrate on your breathing. Take ten slow, deep breaths with your diaphragm, and feel yourself return to a calmer state.

Once again, here are some of the benefits of meditation:

- Creates happiness.

- Attracts positive people and situations into our lives.

- Boosts our immune system.

- Strengthens our positive emotions.

- Develops optimism.

- It reduces the need to be materialistic.

- It increases spirituality.

- Helps you become more creative.

- It helps you boost your self-esteem.

- It helps you become less self-centered.

- Dramatically improves your sleep.

- Helps regulate blood pressure.

- Helps you live longer.

- It helps attract you to positive situations and people, as like always attracts like. Once you start to meditate, you will notice that you will want to take better care of your body and mind. This is a very common benefit of meditation.

- It reduces the feeling of envy.

- Improves relationships.

- And the list goes on and on.

Ask yourself, where in the world would you find all these benefits in a pharmaceutical drug? The answer is you cannot! Meditation is one of the most beneficial forms of all healing. You need to make this a daily practice. No excuses.

In fact, the very first thing you should do before getting out of bed each morning is to take a minute or two and think about some of the things in your life that you can be grateful for. This not only rests your mind and robs the opportunity for you to think about any kind of negative thoughts, but it also changes your brain chemistry to reflect the memory and vibrational frequency of a thought that triggers joy in you. By thinking about something you are grateful for, it not only relaxes the mind and body, but also triggers the release of endorphins. Endorphins are the "good-feeling" chemical. This reduces stress and anxiety. All from thoughts!

Many people have sleeping issues because of their overactive minds during the night. Meditation is a must for them at night. But in addition to meditation, a very important practice is to make your day as interesting as you possibly can. Do new things. Meet new people. Work on a different hobby. Visit different locations. When you make your day different, you become a curious person in a new environment. When your day is different and interesting, you become more present and do not give your mind a chance to wander off thinking negative thoughts. This will calm your thoughts throughout the day and by the time you go to bed at night, you will not only be exhausted from the busy day, but your mind will also be at ease and will help you fall asleep faster.

Meditation is a must if you want to reduce stress and anxiety, and eliminate yourself from depression.

Affirmations

Affirmations are such an important part of our overall health. Affirmations are sentences or words that we say to ourselves. These positive words are changing our thought pattern and changing our mood.

The next time you feel stressed; take a few deep, slow breaths, and repeat, "I am love. I am peace. I am harmony." Remember, the brain does not know the difference between something that is actually happening and when you think thoughts about something happening. So, if you are saying or thinking, "I am love. I am peace. I am harmony," the brain believes that you are indeed love, peace, and harmony, and then releases the chemicals from the brain and throughout the body that coincide with that affirmation. Depending on the level of stress you are experiencing at the time depends on how many times you have to repeat these affirmations to start to calm down. Obviously, the greater amount of stress that you are experiencing, the more affirmations you will have to repeat.

The subconscious mind's main duty is to protect us. It does trillions of things to our sixty+ trillion cells every single second. It exists to keep us alive. It makes our heart beat, controls our body core temperature, and does trillions of other things every second to make sure we are alive and well. Ask yourself what sometimes happens when you are in a very dangerous situation. Maybe you are out on the ocean in a small boat when a storm picks up. You all of a sudden start to say, even without knowing that you are saying it, "It's going to be okay. It's going to be okay. It's going to be okay." This is your subconscious mind working the way it should, as a defense mechanism to try to calm you down. The more you say it, the calmer you will feel.

Affirmations have the potential of completely transforming someone's life if used in the right way and frequent enough. If you have the chance to record yourself saying affirmations, do it. Play these affirmations while you sleep, during your entire sleep. You will not consciously hear the affirmations while you sleep, but your subconscious mind will record every single word that it hears.

Just because your conscious mind does not hear or see things, does not mean that your subconscious mind doesn't.

Remember, the conscious mind can register about 2,000 bits per second, while your subconscious mind can register over 400 billion. That's how subliminal advertising works. In a subliminal ad, the viewer or listener does not register the actual message, because it flashes on the screen too quickly. But the subconscious mind sees everything, no matter how quickly it flashes on the screen. In subliminal ads, the message bypasses your conscious awareness and sinks into your subconscious mind. Subconscious ads are so effective that they are banned in several countries.

Most of us are brought up in a society where we believe that if we are not worrying over the health or wellbeing of someone that we care about, we are doing something wrong. Let's take for example that your wife is about to have surgery. You are in the waiting room pacing the floor, biting your nails, and trying not to engage in any conversations with your family members that are trying to take your mind off the situation. Most people would believe that if you are not worrying about your family member who is about to have surgery, then you simply just don't care. We have to look at the reality of what worrying does to not only weaken the immune system of the person worrying, but how it affects everyone in the room.

When we are worrying, we start to breathe shallowly. When we start to breathe shallowly, we start to trigger the release of cortisol from our adrenal gland, which then stresses us out and causes anxiety. All this is coming from thoughts, nothing else. In this case, the thoughts are anticipatory thoughts about the future, as in, *I hope nothing bad happens to my wife during surgery*. While a family member or someone that we love is in

CHAPTER 10 Top things to do to reduce stress and anxiety.

any kind of distress and we cannot directly help in any way, just like in the case of waiting for a loved one to get out of surgery, one of the very best things we can do is to meditate on exactly what we want to see happen.

When we meditate and visualize what we want to see happen, we are sending that visualization out into the universe. So let's take, for example, that while your partner is having surgery, you not only do not worry, but you enter a state of meditation and visualize your partner completely healthy and that the surgery went great. You are actually contributing to your partner's success, because we now know that our subconscious mind is connected to other people's subconscious mind. In fact, we are all connected. The idea of separateness is merely just illusion. So, when you consciously visualize your partner completely healthy, the subconscious mind of your partner actually picks up on this and registers those thoughts. And remember, the brain does not know the difference between something real and something thought of, so their brain registers what you are visualizing and actually contributes to their healing. Some people refer to this as prayer and the universal consciousness (the connectedness that is omniscient, omnipotent, and ever present, always was, always will be) as God.

Do you ever notice what happens when a toddler is running around and he falls down? The child looks up at mom, and the mom looks down at the child. The child is considering crying but not totally sure. He's thinking, "Well, it is sore but I don't think that I have to cry at this point." Mom is still looking to see whether the child is going to cry. The child is holding it in at this point, and doesn't look like he is going to cry, but as soon as the mother runs over and shows concern the child starts to cry. Why? The concern of the mother influenced the baby not only to react but also to feel the pain even more.

Consider again, the placebo effect. When the brain holds thoughts that a sugar pill is actually a real pill designed to address the illness, the brain releases all the chemicals and hormones to address the symptoms of the illness. Well, when you visualize your partner in complete health, their subconscious mind recognizes this and their brain reacts. That is why group meditations are so effective in the recovery of someone going through an illness. The more people that are meditating and visualizing the person in perfect health, the more effective it is because the subconscious mind of the person, who is experiencing the illness, is picking up on all the visualizations of the group.

Obviously, the most important person in this equation is the one suffering the illness themselves. If their conscious and subconscious mind holds the belief they are not going to recover from the illness, the subconscious mind will see to it that their beliefs become reality. But when the sufferer's mind and the minds of the people doing the group meditation are all aligned, and everyone is visualizing the sufferer in perfect health, this can actually lead to a much quicker recovery time.

When a loved one is suffering with an illness or having surgery, most loved ones do exactly what they should not be doing. They worry, fear the worst, and anticipate negative news from the doctor. Keep in mind the subconscious mind of the person in surgery or with the illness can pick up on everything you are thinking. If you fear the surgery is not going to be a success, your love one's mind is registering these thoughts and their brain is reacting according to what you are thinking.

I once heard someone say, "Worry is a prayer for what you don't want." This statement is completely accurate. This is why we have to wake up to how the mind and brain works. It is totally okay to not worry about someone in pain or suffering. This does not mean to totally avoid the situation. If you can help, help. If you can be of assistance, assist. All I am saying is that pacing the floor and constantly worrying about the health of someone else is actually going to send that vibrational frequency out into the universe, and the sufferer is going to pick up on it.

Now you're thinking, "Well what if my wife is in surgery and my family sees me downstairs laughing up a storm while I am waiting for her to get out of surgery. They are going to think that I don't care." Well, do you care? The answer is that you care so much that you are not allowing what other people think of you to interfere with what you know is the right thing to do. Remember, if you are caring what other people think of your positive behavior, you are allowing your ego and thoughts to get the best of you. If they want to judge you for your behavior, it is a reflection of them, not you.

Worrying attracts more things into your life that trigger stress and anxiety. Meditation heals. Period.

Catching your negative thoughts

In this section, I would like to introduce you to probably one of the most important parts of this entire book. If you practice what this section has to offer, you can completely transform your life, rid all of your unnecessary stress and anxiety, and start to attract amazing things into your life.

As I previously mentioned, most people are on autopilot every day and not even aware of it. This is also known as being "unconscious." This is not the same meaning as being in a coma and being unconscious. In this context, being conscious means that you are aware of your surroundings and the way things really are. But when you are unconscious, you are just going by day to day and allowing your thoughts to rule your life, cause you years of needless stress and anxiety. Most of all, living day to day unconsciously means that you believe you are the victim of your circumstances. A conscious person realizes that they are the creator of their reality and that their thoughts create who they are, what they are becoming, and exactly what they attract. You can also replace the word "unconscious" with "asleep" and "conscious" with "awake."

If you are experiencing chronic stress or anxiety, this means you are allowing your thoughts to get the best of you and you are living unconsciously. For instance, you could be doing work on your computer and just go through the motions, while your thoughts are going a million miles a minute. You are thinking about who your ex-girlfriend is with, what your boss is going to do because of your mistake on the accounting documents, or whether you are going to lose the mortgage on your house because your company is on the verge of downsizing. This is what it means to live unconsciously.

Here is what I want you to do. I want you to try your best to catch when this is going on. When what is going on, you ask? When your thoughts are getting the best of you and thinking all kinds of negative thoughts. You could be taking out the trash and your mind is filled with hundreds of negative thoughts shooting off one by one. Try to catch when this happens. When you catch yourself thinking negative thoughts, something amazing happens! When you catch yourself thinking negative thoughts, you become present, still, and calm, because it is impossible to catch yourself thinking negative thoughts and think negative thoughts at the same time. In the moment of catching your negative thoughts, you are actually meditating. And remember what happens when you are meditating? You cannot think negative thoughts at the same time. So as soon as you catch yourself thinking negative thoughts, you relax for even a split second. Now what is going to happen about two seconds after you catch yourself thinking negative thoughts? Well, most likely you are going to get caught right back into the egotistic realm of negative thinking. This is okay! It takes time and practice. When you start to enter the realm of negative thinking, you will not even notice that you are thinking negative thoughts because you are so used to it. It has become your normal way of living over the years.

The more you catch your negative thoughts; two things will inevitably start to happen:

You will start to notice that you are not your thoughts. You will start to view your thoughts as the external entity that is trying to take over and occupy your mind. This entity is your ego and your ego is not you. When you were born into the world, you were pure innocence, pure consciousness. When you started to grow older, you developed the ability to think to the point where you started to fill your mind with thousands of lies, inaccurate perceptions, and millions of negative thoughts. This was never and will never be who you are. This is your ego. The ego survives when you are not aware that you have an ego. Remember, being unconscious means that you are not aware of the ego. The second that you become aware, by catching your negative thoughts, the ego ceases to exist for that moment. The ego cannot exist when you are aware of the present moment. When you hear a sound and know that you are hearing a sound, the ego cannot exist. When you see a street sign and register that street sign, then the ego cannot exist. This is called, "awareness." The more you catch your negative thoughts, the more you will start to realize that your ego is your negative thoughts and you are certainly not your ego.

The better you become at catching your negative thoughts, you will inevitably start to smile at your ego. You will play with it. Picture a mouse trying to sneak up on a piece of cheese in the corner of your living room, with your cat sitting on the couch. You are the cat and the mouse is your ego. The mouse (ego) slowly creeps into the room and as soon as the cat (you) becomes aware of the mouse, the mouse disappears, running back into the hole in the wall. Your ego will try to sneak back into your mind as negative thoughts. Once you get used to catching the ego, you will start to play around with it and smile, saying to yourself, "No, no, not this time!"

Catching your negative thoughts on a regular basis will put you in mini states of meditation. While you are in these states of mini meditation periods, your mind is relaxed, calm, still, and at peace. During these periods, you don't feel stress or anxiety. The more you do this the better you become. Because you are experiencing meditation periods, you automatically boost your immune system, regain energy, and realize that you are not your thoughts.

When you do this enough, you become so good at it that presence becomes your predominate state of living. When presence becomes your predominate state of living, you start to live a life that you previously thought was not possible.

This one technique can rid you of a life of unneeded stress, anxiety, and depression.

Nature

Have you ever been stressed out and felt the urge to just get away from what you were doing, whether that be work on the computer, in the middle of an argument with your spouse, or even house chores? So, you decide to go for a walk out in nature, maybe a trail in the woods or a walk around the lake. Why is this calming? Why do you feel so tranquil when you do this?

Stepping away from what is triggering stress in your life is so important. We were not born to sit all day watching TV, listening to the radio, or on social media websites. Our bodies are meant to move. Experiencing nature calms the mind and the body for one very important reason. Nature does not have thoughts. Nature does not have an ego. You know that no matter how bad of a day you are having, nature will not judge you, ridicule you, or make fun of you in any way. Nature is amazingly present. It does not think; therefore, it does not have an ego.

This is why nature has a calming effect on the mind and body. When you are in the presence of a non-egoistic entity, it automatically calms you, because energy that we are in the presence of will affect us. Just like being in the presence of a cute dog calms us, or being around a laughing baby makes our day seem lighter. This is happening because babies and dogs do not think like adult humans. Their minds are not full of dwelling on negative things in the past or fearing what could happen in the future. They are present. They are still. We feel that from them subconsciously, and it affects us by calming us.

Another huge part of getting out in nature is the oxygenating effect that clean, fresh oxygen has on our health and well-being. Most people have no idea how much of an impact that clean oxygen has on our health. Oxygen is one of the primary catalysts for energy, health, and wellbeing in the human body. Not only does oxygen keep us alive, but also it plays a role in every metabolic process that a human being experiences. Healthy cells in the body are aerobic, meaning that they require a particular amount of oxygen for cellular reparation and growth. When the body is lacking a sufficient amount of oxygen, decay sets in and cells can mutate or actually die.

CHAPTER 10   **Top things to do to reduce stress and anxiety.**

When you go out and walk around in nature, be present. Look around you and notice many things that you have not noticed before. The second that you register something new means that your total awareness is on that one thing, and guess what, you are meditating! Remember, meditation simply means that your total focus is on what is going on right now, in this moment. When you are focused on what is going on right now, you cannot think about anything else. When you cannot think about anything else, you obviously cannot think any negative thoughts. And seeing that stress and anxiety are caused from negative thoughts, you are automatically going to reduce the amount of stress and anxiety in your life.

Walk around and take notice of absolutely everything that you can. Feel your feet touch the ground; notice how hard the ground feels or the grass touching your toes. Step for step; notice what you are walking on. If there are trees around you, go touch them. Smell them. Feel them. Hug them. When you smell the scent from a tree and notice how it smells, you are meditating. Notice how the crisp air feels on your skin. Don't' think about it. Feel it. Touch the grass with your hands and run your toes through it. Don't worry what other people think of you while you are doing this. Remember, if you do care about what other's think that is your ego talking.

While you are doing all of this, try to be conscious of your breath. Breathe slowly in through the nose and then out through your mouth. Breathe with your diaphragm, not with your chest as we talked about earlier. We are supposed to breathe this way. It allows more oxygen to enter the body. When we breathe slowly, we reduce cortisol release and boost the immune system.

Make sure that you are going for at least one walk a day. It not only gets your blood flowing, but it exposes you to sunlight, clean oxygen, and stills your mind. This is vital in reducing stress and anxiety. Most people know how beneficial a nice walk outside is, but most people don't do it. Don't be one of those people.

Pick the right friends

If you want to become a good baseball player, are you going to continue to play a team that is not as good as you? Of course not! If you continue to play a team that is not as good as you, you would have no reason to push yourself to become better. You can play at 70% of your best and still beat them. You would never strive to become all you are meant to be. In fact, you may even lose your skill. If you don't practice something that you are good at, you will eventually lose that ability.

The same holds true for the people that you hang around. You become who you are around most. Imagine walking into a room and you are having a great day. Then in the corner, you see someone with their head down, shoulders drooping, and you know they are depressed. How is that going to affect your mood? It will be like a slap in the face and drain you of all your excitement, passion, and energy. Remember, this person is not draining you; neither is his depression draining you. It's your thoughts about his essence that is draining you. Imagine the exact opposite situation. One day you are not having the best day. You walk into a room and you are greeted by a huge smile from your friend. This automatically, even on a minuscule level, triggers that little spark in you.

Now imagine if you have a friend or friends in your life that are constantly pessimistic, concentrating on all the wrong in this world. Sentence after sentence from them is negative. How do you think this is going to make you feel? Your thoughts are affected and will always drain you of your energy and decrease your mood. It will also lower your immune system and can even start to trigger the release of cortisol in you. Most people have no idea how negative some of their friends are because they are so used to this. They grew up with these people and they don't know them any other way. And because this is their normal, they have no idea how much they are being affected by it.

In order to see how negative some of your friends are, you really have to step away from them for quite some time. After reentering their lives, on any capacity, you will then notice how much they drain you. It is like eating very healthy, completely organic for five years. Then one day you go to a fast food restaurant and eat a huge greasy meal. Your body would reject it so fast and you would become, most likely, very ill, and very fast. It's because you are not used to the unhealthy food anymore. But you wouldn't have had this adverse reaction if you were the type of person that ate unhealthy every now and then, because your body would have been used to it.

It takes being away from the toxicity in order to see how toxic people and situations can be sometimes. Once again, there is nothing wrong with gently exiting certain people's lives. We need to understand this as a society. If your friends are constantly dragging you down, find new friends. Sometimes the people who drag us down are not so easy to get away from, such as our family members. That's okay, and sometimes we cannot completely exit their lives. That does not mean we have to be there with them as much as we used to be, day and night, in every social event or activity. People and situations that you are in the presence of will affect you. You have to choose very wisely who you hang out with. We are talking about your health. There is nothing more important.

Take care of yourself by choosing who enters your life.

Realizing things don't make you happy

Nothing you can buy will ever make you happy. Things give the illusion that you are experiencing happiness, when in fact; the newness of the thing occupies your mind. When something is occupying your mind, that means your mind and ego do not have the ability to think negative thoughts.

By the time the newness wears off the thing you purchased, you start to feel the stress again. This happens time and time again, when people feel the urge to go on a vacation or move away. They think the place they are living in is causing them stress and anxiety. They think that all their problems will be solved by moving out of the state, province, or country. And when they move, they do indeed feel better, for the first few weeks or months, that is. During the first few months, they are getting to know the new place. They are meeting new people and just learning to get around the new city. All of this newness is occupying their mind and not allowing their mind

CHAPTER 10   **Top things to do to reduce stress and anxiety.**

to concentrate on the negative thoughts that typically occupy their mind on a daily basis. But what happens when the person gets to know the city pretty good and then can drive around practically unconsciously, like most people drive around? Then their mind does not have to be looking for every street sign or landmark, this gives the ego its opportunity to start thinking up all those negative thoughts all over again. And the person becomes trapped back in their old way of thinking. After a few months of stress again, they think the city did not do as much as expected. But what they have to realize is things or places do not cause you stress or happiness. You cause your stress or happiness. Sometimes getting away from the city or place that you live is great. It gives you different scenery, a fresh start, and maybe some extra sun and heat. And there is absolutely nothing wrong with desiring a vacation or a different place to live. The problem occurs when you think the move is going to take all your stress and anxiety away. Remember, stress and anxiety come from your thoughts, not from places or situations. Your thoughts have to change, not necessarily the situation or place that you live in.

You create your stress and anxiety by your reaction to things. You can take it away by changing your reaction (thoughts).

Exercise

We are not meant to sit inside the house all day watching TV or wasting our time on social media. The body is meant to move, and move a lot! People who existed hundreds of years ago did not suffer with the staggering rates of stress and anxiety that people suffer with nowadays. One of the biggest reasons why is because they were active, hunting their food, planting their crops, and doing day to day things that kept them alive. We don't have to do these things now because the technological era has made life too easy for us.

They moved, and they moved every day. These people spent most of their time outside, in fresh air, without all the pollution that we experience now in bigger cities. They super oxygenated their bodies with clean air and their minds were occupied on doing the things they had to do on a daily basis that ensured their survival. Now, we have the ability to become so lazy because everything is given to us. We don't have to grow our own crops; all we have to do is walk to the corner store to buy food. We don't have to walk a mile to the closest well to fetch our water; we now have the ability and comfort to walk five feet to the nearest faucet.

Yes, the technological era brought some great benefits, but it has also made us lazy. The human body is made to move every single day. Regular exercise has been proven to reduce stress, anxiety, depression, boost self-esteem, and improve sleep. It also strengthens your heart, energy levels, regulates your blood pressure, reduces body fat, and overall makes you live a healthier life. You are never going to find those types of benefits in a pill.

Exercising is an absolute must when it comes to defeating stress, anxiety, and depression. However, the very last thing a clinically depressed person wants to do is exercise. I am not suggesting that you try to transform your entire life overnight. That is unrealistic. But you need to learn to take baby steps.

Go for a brisk five-minute walk. You don't have to start with an hour in the gym. The more you do these baby steps, the more energy you get back every day, and the more ambition you have to continue to exercise. Exercising also gives you back the energy you need to do other things that will get you back on the right track.

We need to move our bodies, every day. This reduces stress and anxiety more than you can ever imagine.

Avoid trying to be right

Are you ever in the presence of a few friends, family members, or co-workers and you know deep down that what is being talked about is wrong. You have this burning desire to prove them wrong. You know what you know to be true and you can't wait to talk over their voices and show them you have information they do not.

Voicing your opinion, in many situations, is the right thing to do. It can be proactive and result in positive change. This is not what I am referring to. I am referring to the ego's need to be right, not in just one situation, but all situations. The ego's main concern is to be right, not necessarily the change or improvement that comes from speaking the truth, but simply put, the need to be right. Being right to the ego means that you know something other people do not. You know more information; you are smarter; and you have something they do not, the right answer.

Have you ever tried to convince someone of something you know is true and the person that you're trying to convince simply doesn't believe it? But it's so important to you that they see it from your eyes, from your point of view. Well, sometimes it's important that they try to see things from a different perspective, but only if this results in productive transformation, and not just an elevation of your ego. If you know something to be right and are in the midst of an argument about it, don't allow your ego to win. Your ego loves the heated debate. Your heart beats faster. You start to breathe shallower, and of course, you start to release the stress hormone, cortisol. All of this is attracting and developing stress and anxiety, and of course, weakening your immune system.

If you're trying to prove a point because it will be helpful to someone or a particular situation, then yes, try your best to prove that what you are saying is indeed true. Most people need to be right just to be right. Their goal is not to be productive or to try to help someone with the new information; it is simply to be right.

The next time you have the opportunity to enter or maintain a heated debate, I challenge you to step back and not allow your ego to win. Say to your counterpart, "you're probably right." Watch his/her ego deflate and witness the heated debate suddenly turn into a rational conversation. Continue to do this over and over again with the people in your life that love to debate. It's like not giving attention to an adolescent bully. The more you ignore the bully the less he wants to bully you.

You will notice that once you let go the urge to always be right, your relationship with your partner, friends, family, and co-workers becomes calmer, more rational, and more genuine. Show your ego who is boss by being aware of it. Awaken yourself, feel the freshness of life, and stop being trapped by an egotistical mind. You control everything by the thoughts you think. Take ownership of these thoughts and don't allow these thoughts to rule you.

Eating clean

As we talked about earlier, what we eat affects who we are, our mood, and practically every level of our health. As noted earlier, most people don't eat real food anymore. They eat food-like products created in a laboratory and sold as chemicals, not food.

I won't talk a lot about clean eating, as I talked about it earlier. But just keep in mind that when shopping for food, shop for fresh food. Your goal is to eat food with one ingredient, not a multitude of ingredients that you cannot pronounce. These ingredients are chemicals, not food!

Eat what was available 500 years ago and not what is being mass marketed and produced. This is the key to eating healthy.

Be careful what you say!

We all use words in some form. We talk, text, email, and think. In fact, as mentioned earlier, we have on average about 60,000 thoughts a day. Most of these thoughts, for the average person, are negative thoughts. They either dwell on something negative that happened in the past or fear something that could happen in the future. This triggers the release of cortisol, produces shallow breathing, and creates stress and anxiety.

We have talked many times in this book about thoughts. Let's talk about words and the power that words hold, whether we say them out loud, think them, or write them down. Every word that we think or say holds a particular vibrational frequency. Every word holds energy. For instance, if I were to look at you and say the word, "love," it will affect your mind, thoughts, and immune system a particular way, because you know what love means. You have experienced love, and you know the way it makes you feel. Love is the feeling you felt holding your newborn for the first time. Love is what you feel when your pet dog runs to greet you after you have experienced a stressful day at work. Love is the feeling you have when you say, "I do," at the altar. You know what love means and you feel, even if only slightly, the effects of this word on your body when you hear or say it.

Now let's say I walked up to you and out of the blue said the word, "cancer." Oh, no! You know what this word means. You may have had a family member that has died from cancer and all of a sudden feel like a little of your energy drained. This is completely normal, as every word we say or think, holds a particular energy to it.

Most people are saying words on a day-to-day basis that not only drag them down, weakening their immune system, but also affect the person they are talking to. Think about this. What do a lot of people say when asked, "How are you today"?

You often hear the reply, "Not bad." Remember, the brain does not know the difference between something that is actually happening and when you think about the same thing. In this case, the brain hears, "bad." We know what this word means and our body reacts to it. Another example would be when a person says, "Thank you so much for your help." A person's reply might be, "No problem." Remember, the brain hears, "problem" and the body reacts to exactly what it hears, 100% of the time. Another popular response is, "Don't worry about it," when someone says, "I appreciate your help."

I am going to challenge you from this day forward. I want you to hold yourself accountable and teach this to your friends and family. The next time someone asks you, "How are you?" Don't say, "Not bad." Flip the terminology around and basically say the same thing with a positive spin. Instead of saying, "Not bad," say, "Pretty good," or "Great!" Instead of replying, "No problem," when someone says, "Thank you," say what you really mean, "You're welcome." Instead of saying, "Don't worry about it," or, "No worries," when someone says they appreciate what you have done for them, say what you really mean, "My pleasure." Although you may be thinking that something as simple as this will not affect the level of stress and anxiety you experience, it does.

Remember, very rarely does one big, traumatic experience cause prolonged stress and anxiety. Dozens of little things that we do on a daily basis triggers the release of cortisol (the stress hormone) that creates stress and anxiety.

Change the multitude of little things you do every day

and watch your life change in ways that you could not have imagined possible.

The appreciation factor

Most do not give thanks for the roof over their heads until they get a leak. Most do not give thanks for the food they eat until they cannot afford to buy groceries. Most do not give thanks for their family until they suffer the loss of a loved one. One does not give thanks for their employment until they are laid off. In fact, it's seen regularly that the people of abundance complain about exactly what they would appreciate once lost. Most complain about the taste of healthy food, the stress at work, the annoying family member, and the small house they live in. All of this would change once they lost it.

A very important element that cannot be neglected while talking about struggle and resilience is what happens after one gets through the struggle naturally and comes out on the other side. When someone effectively gets through a struggle, a sense of appreciation is achieved. This appreciation would not have been experienced if the struggle did not exist. We live in a society where most do not give thanks for their current health until it is taken away from them. This fact forces one to enter a state of appreciation once the struggle has ended. This level of appreciation would not have existed without the struggle. Depending on the severity of the struggle, the level of appreciation will vary. For instance, the level of appreciation that is experienced when one overcomes the flu is a lot less from one that beats cancer.

CHAPTER 10   **Top things to do to reduce stress and anxiety.**

When one appreciates without being forced

When one appreciates, one is healing. Gratitude is crucial in recovering from any illness. In a lot of cases, illness cannot exist when one is appreciative of all the things in one's life. For instance, if one were in complete appreciation and feeling gratitude of one's body, would that person feed it toxins in the form of alcohol, drugs, processed food, etc.? If that person were completely aware of the damage those toxins can do to the body, they would appreciate their body enough to not do this. By taking care of the body, the way it is meant to be taken care of, illnesses associated with poor diet cannot exist.

A person cannot live life without experiencing appreciation. But the fact of the matter is, you have two choices. You can learn to appreciate and be thankful for what's in your life right now or you can allow nature to force appreciation upon you by taking it away.

If you don't appreciate your body and are constantly feeding it toxins, nature is going to kick in and make you sick. While experiencing sickness, you will want to become healthy again; this health could have been achieved if you would have appreciated your body to begin with and not fed it toxins. Appreciation for the body first would tell nature to back off, because you don't need a kick from it to smarten you up. It's either you appreciate your body first or nature will force you to appreciate it later. It's your choice. But the magic happens when you appreciate it without being forced. Here you build commitment, dedication, awareness, presence, and vision.

If you don't appreciate your car enough to be changing the oil when it needs changing, eventually your car is going to break down and force you to appreciate what your car has been doing for you all along. It's your choice. Schedule regular oil changes for your car. Appreciate it now, or allow nature to take its toll and cause the car to break down, forcing you into a state of appreciating having a car that works.

If you don't appreciate your partner enough by showing love, compassion, honesty, and forgiveness, nature will kick in and that partner will eventually become tired of the relationship. And of course, when that person walks out on the relationship, that loss is felt. If appreciation for the partner would have been experienced to begin with, love, compassion, honesty, and forgiveness would be characteristics of the person who is appreciating their partner and the partner would not have left.

So many "struggles" can be avoided in life when one shows true appreciation first. Once again, you always have the choice. You can show appreciation first or you can allow nature to show you that you should have been appreciating to begin with. Trust me when I say, it's always better to show appreciation first.

Let's look at some benefits to feeling appreciation:

- Being in a regular state of gratitude will make you a happier person.
- Will boost your immune system.

- Will help attract more positive people into your life.

- Makes us become more present, nicer, and social.

- Improves relationships.

- Reduces pain.

- Improves sleep and sleep quality.

- Improves work relationships.

- Makes you more optimistic.

- Makes you less materialistic.

- Improves self-esteem.

- Helps you become more spiritual.

- Helps you become less envious.

- Less self-centered.

- Heightens your resilience levels.

So why not begin with gratitude? Why not tell nature that she doesn't have to kick in and force you to appreciate the things in your life by taking them away from you? Why not experience all the benefits that come along with showing gratitude first?

You cannot feel gratitude and complain at the same time. Choose gratitude.

Don't take things personally

Although all the lessons and techniques in this book are important to practice to reduce stress and anxiety, implementing this one technique and understanding alone has the potential to completely transform your life.

There are a lot of books that have been written on the subject of presence and meditation. Presence, as we described earlier, is vital in achieving balance, health, and wellness. But we have to understand something. Yes, meditation is great and practicing presence is vital in calming the mind. What about when you are going through a great deal of stress because of your reaction to something very traumatic that happened in your past? Yes, meditation is very helpful in calming your mind, but the reality is that your trigger still exists. Let's say you caught your best friend of twenty years hitting on your spouse. You feel betrayed and your thoughts about this betrayal are getting to you more and more every day. You slowly slip into the grip of anxiety and you fear that it could eventually lead you down a road of depression. Meditation will absolutely help rest your mind and practicing presence will help calm your mind, emotions, and body. But the trigger (your thoughts about the betrayal) is still very alive, lying dormant, waiting for you to slip into another stressful situation. And then, when you guard is down, it will grab you without warning and possess your mind.

So how do we get rid of the thoughts that are lying dormant, just waiting to attack you again when you feel vulnerable? It's not so much that we have to get rid of the thoughts. It's a matter of understanding why the situation happened in the first place.

CHAPTER 10   **Top things to do to reduce stress and anxiety.**

Once we understand why the situation happened, we start to look at the situation with a different set of eyes. When we start to understand it from a different perspective, the negative thoughts about the situation lose their ability to create stress in us.

As I mentioned earlier in this book, I speak at events all around the world, showing people how to reduce anxiety. I also speak at a lot of corporate events. One issue I tend to hear from the employees is that they have to work with a person that is constantly "making" them stressed out. Notice how "making" is in quotations marks. Obviously, the very first thing I have to help them understand is that their co-worker is not causing them to experience stress; it's their reaction to their co-worker that is causing them to experience stress. I also hear at my public presentations all kinds of stories afterwards about why people suffer with stress and anxiety. I hear, all the time, "My kids are stressing me out." "My parents are stressing me out." "My boss is stressing me out." Well, once again, I help them understand it's not any of those things stressing them out, but their reaction to those things.

But this is what is vital to understand. When someone is trying to get under our skin, annoy us, insult us, or just trying to cause pain, we need to understand that when we start to take this personally, we are giving up our power. If someone has a problem with you, it is vital to understand; they have the problem, not you. Just look at the structure of the sentence, "They have a problem with you." They are the ones with the problem, not you. But the second you take offense to their problem, it becomes your problem.

151

You may be saying this is easier said than done, and you are quite right. There is a crucial step that you must take before being in a position to not take things personally. That step is to understand how the human mind works. Once you understand how the mind works, you will be in a position where understanding replaces anger, and pity replaces hatred for the person trying to get under your skin.

In order to understand this step, let's examine free will. Free will is the belief that we have the ability to do and act the way we please. But research is showing us that over 90% of the time, we do not pick our desires, cravings, or urges. These desires, cravings, and urges come from the beliefs that we hold predominately in our subconscious mind. What am I trying to say? I am telling you that well over 90% of the time, you, and the person that is treating you unfairly are on autopilot. If the person that is treating you unfairly is on autopilot, they cannot really change their behavior. And in a way, it is truly not their fault for why they act the way they are acting. I am not saying they should not be held responsible for their actions. They should. When we really look at how the human brain works, we realize it is our subconscious beliefs that have been shaped since childhood that are responsible for the way we act and what we desire now. In other words, our free will is kind of just an illusion.

If you believe that you always have the ability to choose what you want and that you control all of your desires, then think of something you enjoy eating. Think about your favorite food. Once you are thinking about your favorite food, simply snap your fingers and hate it. If you have free will, you should have

CHAPTER 10   Top things to do to reduce stress and anxiety.

the ability to hate your favorite food. The reality is that you still love your favorite food because it is a deep, subconscious belief. Whatever your subconscious mind holds is a belief your body reacts to. Always.

Imagine that if you are at a hypnosis show and you are on stage as a volunteer. The Hypnotist puts you in a trance, which means that your five senses are shut off and your subconscious mind is open to suggestions (things the Hypnotist says). He walks over and implants the subconscious belief that you no longer like ice cream, your favorite desert. You then open your eyes and he displays a bowl of ice cream in front of you. What happens? You are repelled by it. It disgusts you. How can your favorite food now disgust you? It's because you now have a new subconscious belief. That new subconscious belief is that you no longer enjoy the taste of ice cream. Once you snap out of the hypnotic trance, your beliefs return to your regular beliefs, and ice cream is once again your favorite dessert.

Whatever we hold as a subconscious belief becomes our reality. Still don't believe me? Think about something you absolutely hate and simply snap your fingers and love it. Think about a person that you can't stand to be around and suddenly start to love the presence of this person. Think about anything you hate and love it. Think about anything that you love and hate it. You cannot do it, just like the person that is trying to insult you, annoy you, or misbehave around you cannot simply snap their fingers and change what they are desiring to do.

Once again, I am not saying that you should just suck it up and take the emotional or physical abuse. Yes, they should be

153

held responsible. Knowing they are acting on autopilot helps you deal with the situation so much more effectively.

Imagine if your partner accidentally took a poisonous pill that completely changed who he was. He started to insult you, annoy you, and completely change his perception of practically everything. How could you take offense to things he is saying when you know that it's the pill talking, not him? Well that is what is happening with regular people. The huge majority of this world is living completely unconsciously, controlled by their ego and their subconscious beliefs. They simply cannot snap their fingers and change their negative desires, urges, and cravings.

Take, for example, criminals. Do you think they have the ability to simply snap their fingers and change the desire to not want to commit the crime? Of course they don't. Obviously, they need to be held responsible for what they do in some way. But what they need is love, understanding, and rehabilitation, not hatred, hostility, and punishment.

Consider the ongoing issues of bullying in elementary, junior high, and high schools. This is an ever-growing issue that millions of students face every day. One bully bullies another kid. What happens to the bully? The teachers, parents, and administration get together to see what punishment the bully deserves. The teachers, parents, and administration then become the bully! You cannot fight fire with fire and expect to reap positive results. Yes, the bully has to be held responsible but the bully is not in a position (and never was) to change his desires, cravings, and urges. These desires, cravings, and

CHAPTER 10　**Top things to do to reduce stress and anxiety.**

urges were implanted into his conscious and subconscious mind over his entire lifetime, which then created subconscious beliefs. Once they become subconscious beliefs, his personality, moods, and everything that makes him was created. The bully needs understanding, love, and compassion, not ridicule, punishment, and judgment. Until we start addressing the bullying issue the way it is meant to be addressed, we will never solve this ongoing problem.

Most people judge others when they do something "wrong" or "bad." It's important to understand that when you judge someone for what they are doing, you are basically saying that you are better than them. The reality is no one is better than anyone else. We are all the same consciousness, scattered all over the earth, giving the illusion that we are different entities. So, when you judge someone else for what they did, you are really projecting what you are feeling. Judgment is actually a reflection of you and not the person that you are judging. If you had a completely peaceful mind and actually understood that people act in accordance to their subconscious mind's beliefs, then you would realize they are practically on autopilot. If you truly understood this, you would not judge; you would look at them with compassion. But when the mind is occupied with misunderstanding, anger, and rage, you tend to look at other's behavior in a judgmental way. This is why judging is a reflection of your own mind and not another person's "wrongful" doing.

When you look at the most vicious crime committed by a criminal and you feel love towards them because you know they are in a position they did not choose, then that's when you can consider yourself awakened to this principle. When

155

love replaces anger and compassion replaces ridicule, you know that you are starting to understand how the mind works. You can confidently say that you are no longer taking the actions of other's personally.

Everything that you emotionally recognize in someone else is within you. This does not mean that just because you are aware that a murderer lives down the street that you are or will ever become a murderer. There is a difference between recognizing a fact and emotionally being affected by someone else's behavior.

Let's say you pick up the newspaper and read that Tommy from down the street was arrested the day before for physically assaulting his wife. You can react in one of two ways. You can think, "Oh wow, I had no idea that Tommy was experiencing issues. I hope that he gets the help he needs and that his wife is okay." Or, you can think, "That piece of trash, I hope he rots in prison."

With the first reaction, you recognized what he did and realized it is because of his conditioning that he acted in the way he did. You felt pity and concern for him and his wife and hoped he receives what he truly needed, help and rehabilitation. This is a reflection of the type of life you live, and how you perceive situations. In this case, you were understanding and did not allow your ego to get the best of you. In the second reaction, you wished harm upon him. You were not understanding and your ego got the best of you. When the mind does not understand and has been taken over by the ego, this is the type of reaction you will exhibit, a reaction of hostility and vengeance.

CHAPTER 10   **Top things to do to reduce stress and anxiety.**

Exactly what you see in others is always a reflection of yourself.

Controlling the ego can be very difficult when family or a loved one is involved. When a family or loved one is involved in a situation, where the loved one is hurt, abused, or experiencing pain, the ego can take the mind over quite easily. It is so much easier to not allow the ego to take over the mind when something negative happens to a stranger, but when it's someone that we are close to, the ego jumps on board. In order for the person to be aware of the presence of the ego, the mind has to be calm.

Take for example that you and your partner are in an argument. It's a heated fight and emotions are elevated. In order to get anywhere in the argument, our level of rationality and emotions should be balanced. When emotions are through the roof, the level of rationality stays where it originally was and the emotional level out balances your level of rationality. Then it's just ego against ego, fire against fire, and problems cannot be solved this way. This is what Einstein meant when he said, "We cannot solve our problems with the same level of thinking that created them." The ego created the problem, so the ego cannot solve this problem.

When you replace anger and vengeance with love and understanding, you know that you are being awakened to this principle.

157

A different look at Karma

Some people believe the true nature of karma occurs in the "next life." In other words, your next life's experiences, both good and bad, will depend upon the life you previously lived. Others believe that karma occurs in the life you are currently living. For instance, if you do good things, you will attract good into your life. If you do bad things, you will attract bad things/situations.

Although I agree with both schools of thought, I tend to look at karma a little differently. I believe that karma is already in effect before the person does the deed. What do I mean by this?

Well let's take an extreme situation for example, a premeditated murder. Most people will look at a murder and think the murderer, if ever caught, will only see punishment and justice once behind bars. Most people believe if the person is on the run and not caught that he got away scot-free.

So how does karma take effect in the life of a murderer who was never caught? The answer lies within the psychological state of the criminal.

Let's have a look at what's going on in the mind of the criminal before and after he commits such a crime. For someone to commit such a vicious act of hatred, this person (considering he is not completely psychopathic—void of all empathy) has to be suffering from an extreme amount of negativity in his life. In order to have the desire to commit such a crime, hatred, guilt, fear, depression, hostility, envy, anxiety, resentment, shame, and regret have to be dominant forces inside this person's life. And it goes without saying that if these emotions are filling up this person's life, then happiness, joy, compassion, love, gratitude, and peace are all too scarce.

So whether or not the person is caught, he is still attracting a sense of justice into his life. Obviously, authorities should try to constrain someone who is exhibiting such violence, but always rest assured the universe is attracting into his life exactly what he is projecting, even "before" he/she does the deed. The same goes for all the deeds of kindness, love, compassion, and peace. In order for one to exhibit such authentic behavior, he/she must be living that sort of life internally.

You get exactly what you put out. Always. No exceptions.

Visualization and neuroplasticity

Neuroplasticity is not as difficult to understand as it sounds. Neuroplasticity describes how experiences, thoughts, and repetitive behavior reorganize neural pathways in your brain. Remember when we talked about the placebo effect? The placebo effect is a great example of how a new neural pathway is formed; it then changes physiology. If you have an illness and believe you are taking a pill (even though it's a sugar pill) designed to treat the illness, then you create a new neural pathway. This becomes a subconscious belief and of course, the sugar pill acts just like a real pharmaceutical pill.

It was discovered that neuroplasticity could take place at any age. Previously, it was believed that the brain was a physiologically static organ. But now we know that new neural pathways can be created and changed regardless of prior experiences or how you were raised. We now know that subconscious beliefs can change at any age of your life. This is wonderful news because this says that no matter what age you are, you can work on changing and overcome fears, phobias, and anything that triggers stress in you.

If you have a phobia, fear, or if anything triggers stress, this means that you hold a subconscious belief that says whatever you fear is a real fear. If you change your subconscious belief to, "I love dogs," when in fact, you fear dogs, then this will become your new belief and you will no longer have a fear of dogs.

How do you do this? Let's talk about visualization. Remember, the brain does not know the difference between thinking and something real. So, this is where visualization comes into play.

Let's say that you have a fear of flying. I want you to sit in a quiet room and visualize the very first process of flying that triggers stress in you. Maybe this is when you first enter the airport. If you are visualizing correctly, you should start to feel a little uneasiness. This is what I want you to feel. I want you to think about this as vividly as you possibly can. Visualize the people walking around, the luggage in your hand, and the sounds of the airplanes taking off. If you are doing this correctly, you may feel the palms of your hands start to get a little sweaty and you may start to feel a little anxious.

CHAPTER 10   Top things to do to reduce stress and anxiety.

So this is where we are going to change pace. I want you to shake it off and reenter the airport in your mind. But this time I want you to visualize in your mind feeling completely at peace. This will be difficult because you do have a real fear of this process. This may take some time but you will eventually get to a place in your mind where you enter the airport in your mind, feeling great and comfortable. When you master that in your mind, visualize checking in and receiving your boarding pass. Once again, this is going to cause you to feel uneasy again. Get to a place where you can do this in your mind while feeling completely peaceful.

Continue to conquer the fear in your mind step for step until you are actually on the airplane (in your mind) feeling completely peaceful and calm. Here is the secret. When you master this in your mind, you master it in reality, because the brain does not know the difference between something real and something that you are thinking about. So when you build up immunity in your mind, you are actually building up immunity in reality.

This does not necessarily mean you will be completely cured of your phobia the very first time you are exposed to the real thing after you built up immunity in your mind. Maybe this will happen but maybe you will still feel a little anxious. However, you will feel that much better because you have built up immunity during the visualization technique. As you continue to do this, you will completely beat your phobia to the point where your fear just does not exist anymore.

I also want you to start writing down, in present tense, what you want to attract. Write it in present tense because the subconscious mind does not understand what the past or future is. There is only now. Write whatever you want in your life. The brain thinks that whatever you write down, the way you write it, is actually the way it is; so it does it's best to release all the chemicals and hormones into your blood that make your body feel exactly the way it's supposed to feel, to match whatever you are telling it with your writing.

For instance, if you want to attract a more peaceful mind, write down, "I am so happy and thankful that I confront every situation in a very peaceful and loving way." Make this a practice every single day. Write it out as many times as you possibly can. This will help create a new neural pathway in your brain and once this is created, you then hold a new subconscious belief and that belief becomes your reality.

In review...

You need to learn to rest your mind. Negative thoughts create stress and anxiety, which can lead you down a road to depression. When you rest your mind through meditation, you no longer allow your mind the opportunity to think negative thoughts.

Affirmations are a must. This helps create new neural pathways. You probably heard the statement, "Thoughts that fire together, wire together." The more you think particular thoughts, the more chance it has at becoming a new neural pathway, which becomes a new subconscious belief.

CHAPTER 10   **Top things to do to reduce stress and anxiety.**

Catching your negative thoughts means that you are no longer thinking that negative thought. The more you catch them the easier this process becomes and you will start to notice that you are not your thoughts. This can totally transform your entire life and is by far one of the greatest lessons in this book.

Get outside every single day! This is a must. We need fresh air and we need to super oxygenate our bodies. Shallow breathing means cortisol release and cortisol release means that we are going to experience stress and anxiety. Nature calms us. It relaxes us. Don't ever take the healing power of nature for granted.

A friend does not have to be a friend forever. If your friends are constantly dragging you down, it's time to get new friends.

Feeling the need that you have to continue to buy things because it makes you happy is a sign that your negative thoughts are getting the best of you. Buying new things takes your mind off the negative thoughts for a while, until the newness wears off. This is a crutch and you are avoiding what is truly causing your discomfort, your thoughts.

Exercise has been shown time and time again to be one of the greatest ways of reducing stress and anxiety. Exercise outside if you can. It gives you the added bonus of receiving clean, fresh oxygen while you are moving your body. Exercise is a must if you want to reduce stress and anxiety. We are not meant to sit down all day!

You don't always have to be right. If what you're trying to be right about has no real purpose or productive value, don't fight for it, especially when you have no way of proving that you're right. This just grows and develops your ego and causes a heated argument with the person that you are debating with. Simply say, "Yes, you are probably right." Your ego will not like this because it wants fuel to continue the argument. You don't always have to be right.

Eat one-ingredient foods! Period!

Be very careful of what you say, write, text, or email. And especially of what you think. Every word holds a vibrational frequency. Negative words such as sickness, hate, envy, fool, etc. hold a low vibrational frequency. So when you say (or hear) them, you are, even if only slightly, creating stress in your body. When you say positive words such as love, peace, etc., you are raising your immune system. This is why saying and writing affirmations are so important.

Knowing the people that are trying to insult you, get you down, or hurt you do not have the ability to snap their fingers and change their desires is life-changing. It will help you dramatically. When you learn not to take things personally, you experience one of the most liberating feelings that you could ever experience.

Building immunity in your mind to the things or people that trigger stress in you means that you will build immunity in reality. By constantly visualizing what you want to attract into your life, it builds new neural pathways in your brain, which then creates that reality.

CHAPTER 10 Top things to do to reduce stress and anxiety.

Baby steps are the key. Step for step all of these techniques and ways of life will become easier and easier. Like anything, when you keep practicing, it will all become second nature. When it becomes second nature, it becomes your new normal. Then you are transformed.

Chapter 11

How to be grounded.

Although it is important to avoid particular situations (nightclubs, etc.), it is also important to build up immunity to these places. We have to face the facts and realize that no matter how non-toxic we live our lives, we are going to sometimes be confronted with negative people and negative situations. This is just life and it is going to happen.

So, even though it is important to avoid negative situations, we also have to ground ourselves enough to the point where being in these situations does not bother us. So what does grounding mean? Grounding means that you can be in the presence of a negative situation but that negative situation does not affect you. How do you do this? You do this by first realizing that you are about to enter into a negative situation but also realizing that it is your thoughts and reactions to the negative situation that can disturb your peaceful state.

The next time that you are in the midst of a negative situation, let's say you are about to walk into a family gathering where several family members are in a heated argument. Realize that

CHAPTER 11 **How to be grounded.**

you do not have to be a part of it and their negativity will only bother you if you allow it to. No one has the ability to steal your peace of mind unless you give it away. You give it away by entering the debate, arguing back, or by allowing someone to offend you.

When you are about to enter the negative place, visualize yourself in a protective bubble. Any negativity that is thrown your way will automatically bounce off the bubble and not affect you. Although this exercise is a psychological exercise, it is extremely beneficial. Remember, thoughts create your reality. So if you set the intention that you are going to be protected and not bothered, those thoughts are going to protect you and not allow the actions of others to decrease your energy level or affect you in any way.

Simply by setting an intention in your mind programs you for success. Consider any Olympian. They go through constant visualization techniques to be effective in what they set out to do. They picture the end result, holding the goal medal, and being on that pedestal. Setting an intention in your mind tells your brain exactly what you want to happen.

Obviously, when you are first starting to clean up your life, you want to avoid all the toxic environments. It's like an alcoholic trying to avoid triggers that influence him to pick up a drink. Well, the end goal for an alcoholic is to eventually be able to be around triggers and be in a state of mind where the triggers do not affect them anymore.

The same holds true for someone trying to clean up their lives to reduce stress, anxiety, and depression. At first, you should make an effort to avoid toxic situations, environments, and people that trigger stress or toxic thoughts within you. But eventually you want to control your mind enough and take ownership of your entire creation to the point where, if you happen to be in those types of environments, you are completely able to not allow the environment to affect you.

Toxic environments are toxic environments. So you want to avoid them, but there will be some situations where you are in the presence of one. And it is so much better to be able to be in a toxic environment and not allow it to affect you, than to constantly run away from the toxic environment.

It's better to feel peace in the midst of a storm than to constantly run away from it. When you achieve this ability, you are becoming "awakened."

Chapter 12

Quick fixes are not meant to be: the resilience factor.

What happens when you break your leg, have a headache, or stub your toe? What happens when you experience anxiety, stress, depression, or sadness? Of course, you want the discomfort to be gone, not next week, not tomorrow, but right now. And when it takes some time to get back to our normal self, we never think the healing process is fast enough. We typically complain about it in the meantime, only making matters worse. Remember, when you give negative attention, in the form of complaining, to any discomfort in your life, you are only going to amplify the pain.

Let's look at the human body and mind. Although physical pain hurts, and psychological pain hurts, we are designed to absorb these hits. We are designed to suffer through the sorrow. Yes, we are designed to experience the "bad" stuff, the stuff that makes us cry, and the stuff that makes us scream out, "God, why me"? Some people have a very difficult time absorbing this fact. They have a difficult time accepting that life is sometimes not easy. If everyone accepted that life had difficult moments, those moments would be a lot easier to deal with when the time comes.

If we take some time to understand why struggle is important, we will start to not only accept struggle but also embrace it. Struggle is necessary in our lives to build the characteristics we would not have built in the absence of the struggle.

When someone is faced with a struggle of any kind and they effectively get through that struggle without relying on artificial means (drugs, alcohol, etc.), that person creates resilience. Resilience is the person's ability to cope and deal with struggle. How do you build resilience? You build resilience by being exposed to stressful situations and building up immunity to what you're going through. The only way you can build up immunity is to be exposed to these difficult situations.

Imagine trying to become a good hockey player by always playing others that were not as good as you were. They couldn't challenge you. They couldn't put up a fight. How can that make you grow into a better hockey player? It can't. Other players and situations putting you in a difficult situation helps you grow as a hockey player. That's what makes you better. It's by getting through the dreadful 6:00 a.m. practices, the exhausting physical drills, and the endless amount of practice that creates a good hockey player.

You cannot build resilience without going through a struggle. Every struggle is attracted into our lives to help us deal with future struggles more effectively. We need to understand this truth to heal more effectively. The ability to deal with the struggle is determined not by severity of the struggle itself, but by your resilience and perception of it.

Resilience is created from overcoming a struggle in a natural way. You cannot build resilience through alcohol, drugs, food, or anything else that eases the pain temporarily. Using substances to ease the pain will always inevitably make the situation worse, in addition to robbing your ability to create the attributes you would have created if you went through the struggle naturally.

I see so many people try to drink their problems away. While doing this, the mind is artificially numbed by a poison. Human beings are not meant to numb the mind like this. We are not meant to ingest a poisonous substance into us to kill our brain cells and numb the pain of a struggle. When people do this, not only are they ripping apart their physical health, but also they are completely robbing themselves of the opportunities to create resilience. Going through these struggles naturally and overcoming them creates resilience. This is the only way resilience is created.

You cannot numb the mind with a poison and create resilience. And if you try, you will inevitably face your next stressful situation a lot worse, because you have not given yourself the ability to create exactly what you are meant to create while facing struggle. By numbing the mind with a poison, you take away that chance to build up immunity to the struggle you're facing at the time. It's time after time of building up immunity, little by little, that builds the resilience you need as a human being to face future struggles more effectively down the road.

Struggles help us grow. They help us develop. They are there to help us become the person we are meant to be. Masking the pain with a poison will always destroy your chances to create resilience.

Every time you take pain killer meditation for a headache, cough medicine for a cough, or alcohol to relax, you are robbing nature's opportunity to build resilience, not to mention "not" treating the cause of what's causing your discomfort. If you continue to interfere with nature's opportunities to build resilience, you will inevitably face future stressful situations so much more ineffectively.

Resilience is created by facing struggles naturally. Human beings are designed to face struggles, not poison ourselves to numb the pain. Poisoning will always make the situation worse in addition to making you less prepared to face future situations the way you could. You are creating your health by the choices you make.

The reality of pain

Day to day I receive a lot of emails from people suffering from anxiety, depression, psychological abuse, and other related issues. Although I try my very best to respond to everyone, I don't always have the answers they are looking for. But I want to share with you something that I share with many people who approach me for help, and this information always seems to shed some light in their lives.

CHAPTER 12   Quick fixes are not meant to be: the resilience factor.

Think about this: We all suffer from psychological trauma at some point in our lives. Obviously, some people suffer a lot more than others. For the most part, we are taught to believe this "suffering" is bad, negative, and sometimes even evil. But let's think about this for a second.

Present in all of us we have an "inner" invisible intelligence. This intelligence is our subconscious mind. Although terminology may differ with different people, the fact of the matter is that we all possess a magnificent "inner" intelligence. This inner intelligence does not need instructions or commands from us for it to do what it's supposed to do.

This intelligence, day by day, hour by hour, minute by minute is keeping us alive without "us" consciously telling it to. This inner intelligence can handle an estimated 100 trillion instructions per second. Read that again, 100 trillion (that's 100,000,000,000,000). Some of the things this inner intelligence does are flow our blood throughout our veins and arteries, pump just the right amount of blood in and out of our heart, and control our body core temperature, among many other things.

This inner intelligence also governs our estimated 60-100 trillion cells throughout our body. In fact, our cells are doing trillions upon trillion of things every single second. And each cell knows exactly what every other cell is doing instantaneously.

So what's my point? My point is this intelligence is so brilliant that we cannot even start to understand how and why it works. But, we do know the main function of our subconscious mind is to "protect" us. So when you feel like life is too difficult to handle, always know your subconscious mind, and all its magnificent intelligence is throwing situations at you for the "greater good." It would never hurt you for the simple reason for hurting you. It gives us situations because we are ready to grow and without these situations, we cannot. Don't ever challenge the brilliance of our inner intelligence. It knows what we need, when we need it, in the most effective way we need it.

This "inner" intelligence is too brilliant to hurt us for the long run. It's attracting particular situations into our lives for one reason: to help us learn from them, battle through them, and to come out on top appreciating things we could not appreciate without going through the "pain." Always know that although life seems too difficult to handle sometimes, our inner intelligence will only subject us to situations we "can" handle.

Everyone suffers. And if you ever look at someone and envy them for their "perfect," pain-free life, rest assured they too have demons.

Chapter 13

Why do we attract what we attract?

The Law of Attraction is heavily misunderstood by a lot of people. Thousands of people believe that practicing The Law of Attraction simply means visualizing what you want and then holding out your hands to receive it. This is not what the Law of Attraction is, never was, and never will be.

The Law of Attraction holds true that whatever we think about most is what we attract most and also what we are attracted to most. Let's look at some examples.

Let's say you pick up a magazine and read an article about the Red Cross and their efforts to help the hundreds of people affected by a hurricane disaster. A few hours later, you decide to watch some TV and in flicking through the channels, you catch the beginning of a commercial for the Red Cross. Your mind zones in on that commercial, as it is a little more relevant to you because you were just reading an article about it. You may leave the commercial on and watch the entire thing because it was fresh in your mind. You may even want to do a little research on the Red Cross later since it peaks your interest. If you had not read the article hours before, you most likely would have kept channel surfing until you found a decent TV show.

You just joined a fitness facility for the first time in your life. You were never exposed to a gym before. You sign up and are given a tour. Then you start your first work out. On your way home, you realize there are four other fitness facilities on your drive. You didn't notice them before. They never did stand out to you before now. Why? They didn't stand out to you before because you were never exposed to a fitness facility. It was not fresh in your mind. But now that it is, you begin to notice them all around you.

Even though you're not hungry, you become hungry after watching a TV commercial for a fast food restaurant. You get up off the couch and either make something to eat or drive to a fast food restaurant.

Simply put, we are attracted to what we are holding in our minds. But as we now know from reading this book the subconscious mind is the part of the mind that houses our most fundamental beliefs and habits. It's this part of the mind that controls our behaviors and determines what we are attracted to. This part of the mind holds your "true" beliefs and it takes a lot of conditioning to change it.

If we hold the fundamental belief in our minds that we cannot lose weight, well, then our eyes are going to be attracted to all the opportunities that reinforce that belief. Driving downtown our eyes will be more attracted to the fast food restaurants. But what if our fundamental belief in our subconscious mind was,

"I can achieve good health"? Then we'd be more conditioned to drive on the same downtown streets and most likely notice the things that can help us achieve that goal; the fitness facilities, the healthier restaurants, etc.

Whether it is achieving a 90% average in high school, to battling addiction, our minds are attracted to the opportunities that reinforce our most fundamental beliefs about that particular situation.

Although I teach people in my keynotes and workshops, the science of The Law of Attraction and the innermost workings and complicities of the subconscious mind, it doesn't have to be that difficult to understand the true nature of The Law of Attraction.

Although there is a lot more to The Law of Attraction than most people realize the important thing to understand is that we attract and are attracted to what we think about most. Does that mean that we "get" what we think about most. Not necessarily. Once we see the opportunities, we have to act upon them. Most people leave that crucial element out of The Law of Attraction.

But here is the key thing to understand. We can only act upon opportunities that we see. And what we see (what we are attracted to) is heavily determined by what we hold predominately in the back of our minds.

The important thing to understand is that it doesn't really matter if you think, "Hey, I can lose weight," if it doesn't agree with your true belief in the back of your mind (your subconscious mind). The subconscious mind will always win, as this is what you truly believe.

When you are under hypnosis on stage and the hypnotist implants the belief that there is a spider on your arm, your eyeballs actually see a spider on your arm, because that's the new belief in your subconscious mind.

So what happens when we hold the fundamental belief/habit, "I can't fight this addiction, or I can't achieve this university degree"? Our eyes are more attracted to the things that help us live out that belief. The soccer field becomes more attractive than the books and the alcohol becomes more attractive than the soccer field. That's just life. It's real. Always.

Researchers are suggesting that we have approximately 60,000 thoughts a day. The more you think about or are exposed to a particular type of thought, the more it sinks into the back of your subconscious mind and the more it conditions your eyes to see the things that reinforce that particular belief.

What are you thinking about on a regular basis? You cannot change the innermost fundamental beliefs of your subconscious mind overnight. It takes time and work. But it's worth it. It changes your life and in the process, you start to understand how much power you really have to shape your life, if you do it in the way it's meant to be done.

Chapter 14

Resting the mind.

Researchers of the mind are telling us that we have on average approximately 60,000 thoughts a day. Not only are 90% of these thoughts the same thoughts we had yesterday, they are negative thoughts. They are thoughts dwelling on something bad in the past or fearing something that could potentially happen in the future. These thoughts are affecting our stress and anxiety levels. If we are bombarding our minds with negative thoughts, we are actually changing the biochemistry of our brains. If we bombard our minds with negative thoughts we actually cause our hypothalamus (part of our brain) to trigger the release of cortisol from our adrenal gland in our kidneys into our blood. Releasing cortisol into our blood then weakens our immune system, decreases our energy level, inhibits the actions of our white blood cells, and overall just makes us feel depressed.

Remember, our reaction to situations causes stress and anxiety (never the situation itself). What is our "reaction"? Our reaction is our thoughts about the situation. Anger, hostility, jealousy, vengeance, and hatred are all psychological reactions to situations that will ultimately cause stress, anxiety, and could lead you down a road of developing depression.

Think about a thought that makes you feel joy right now. Maybe a beautiful walk on the beach, your wedding proposal, or the first time you laid eyes on your first born. You'll start to feel a comfort come over you when you think these thoughts. In that moment, your brain is actually matching what you're thinking about by secreting "feel-good" chemicals (dopamine, endorphins, etc.) into your blood stream. These chemicals/hormones are actually increasing the effectiveness of your immune system, increasing your energy level, and overall making you feel well.

Now think about something that disgusts you. Maybe your partner cheated on you, or maybe when a friend betrayed your trust. Think about it as if it is happening right now. What do you feel? You don't feel bliss; you don't feel comfort. Your brain starts to match exactly what you're thinking about by triggering the release of cortisol (the stress hormone) into your blood stream, which then creates stress, anxiety, and actually decreases the effectiveness of your immune system. Just from your thoughts!

Resting the mind is one of the most important things we can do to improve our overall health. The mind is not meant to be running all day long and for the most part, it is. It's human nature for the mind to be on autopilot, always thinking day and night. But the mind is like a muscle. It needs rest to work the way it can work. Imagine if you were doing bicep curls. You do one, two, then three and you can't lift the weight four times,

CHAPTER 14 **Resting the mind.**

but you know that if you took a little rest, you would be able to lift that fourth time. Well, the mind works in the same way. In order for it to work the way it is meant to work, you need to give it a rest. The mind (thinking) should be used when you need it; when you need to do something productive—figure out directions, read a book, study, etc. But when you don't need it, it should be put aside. What do I mean by "put aside"? I mean presence, as we have talked about previously in this book. Being present is one of the greatest things that you can do for your health.

Chapter 15

A deeper look at meditation.

Meditation doesn't have to be as complicated or mysterious as people may seem to believe. Meditation simply means turning off your thoughts. For the most part we don't control our thoughts, our thoughts control us. If we did control our thoughts, we would be able to turn off all of our negative thoughts by the snap of our fingers. But we know that is simply not the case.

When someone enters the realm of meditation, the mind is relaxed. It is turned off. Thinking stops, brain waves slow down, and we heal. When there is no thinking, judgment, anger, hatred, jealousy, vengeance, and all the other negative emotions we experience cannot exist. Remember it is emotions like these causing us to feel stressed and anxious. When these emotions are not present, the brain cannot react with the byproduct of these emotions, cortisol, etc. It is here that the mind is completely still, completely at rest, and the person enters a state of healing, a state of regeneration, and a state of consciousness that cannot be achieved with the thinking mind.

CHAPTER 15   **A deeper look at meditation.**

Meditation exists when you concentrate all of your focus on what is going on right now. That's why a lot of people choose to concentrate their focus on their breathing. If you are aware of your breathing and register each and every breath, then you are meditating. You cannot register a breath and be thinking about something in the past or the future at the same time. It's important to keep in mind that when you're meditating, especially when you first start, your mind is not going to want to shut off. Your thoughts are going to drag you off in all kinds of different directions because your mind is not used to being still. Although this is exactly what your mind needs, it's not used to change, and therefore does not want to change.

Keep in mind that when starting out, you're going to notice the mind does not want to enter into meditation. In fact, it's the complete opposite thing it wants to do. Your ego will throw every thought it possibly can to snap you back into thinking. You'll notice that you will go for short periods of time when you are completely absorbed in the present moment, but you'll also notice your mind will quickly snap you back into thinking. Most of the time you will not even notice when you are snapped back into thinking. Then all of a sudden, you will realize the last two minutes that you were thinking again. But the great news is the second you realize this, the second you are aware of your thinking, then you are back into a meditating state. Catching your thinking is success. It means you are becoming aware that your ego is taking over. The more you catch yourself thinking, the more you are meditating.

In today's society we have brainwashed ourselves into thinking the overactive mind is the productive mind. And although we do need our thinking mind to be productive in work, society, and in our leisure time, it is also important to realize that it is even more important to rest our minds. Our minds need rest in order for them to work efficiently. Our minds also need rest because our daily typical thoughts are negative thoughts, full of vengeance, judgment, ridicule, etc. The mind does not enjoy this and it needs to reset.

Resting our minds through meditation has a vast array of benefits:

- Lowers blood pressure.

- Increases blood flow and slows the heart rate.

- Increases serotonin levels, which then influence mood and behavior.

- Can lead to deeper levels of physical relaxation.

- Reduces anxiety attacks by lowering the levels of blood lactate.

- Decreases muscle tension.

- Enhances your immune system.

- Helps promote weight loss.

- Reduces the amount of free radicals.

- Lowers cholesterol.

- Improves airflow to your lungs.

- Can cure headaches/migraines.
- Can reduce the effects of asthma.
- Can improve athletic performance.
- Relaxes your nervous system.
- Can help improve the healing of phobias and fears.
- Helps with focus and concentration.
- Increases creativity.
- Improves learning and memory.
- Increases your feeling of vitality and rejuvenation.
- Increases emotional stability.
- Improves relationships at home and work.
- Develops will power.
- Grows wisdom.
- Helps you connect with your source—regardless of what you believe that it.
- Increases the synchronicity in your life.
- Helps your experience a greater inner-directedness.
- Can even slow down the aging process.

Chapter 16

How to meditate.

If you are new to meditation, this is a quick guide on how you can try it out. Sit in a comfortable chair. Get comfortable but sit relatively erect. Preferably, do not lie down because you run the risk of falling asleep. Make sure you keep your posture straight; having a backrest can help. Don't cross your legs. Keep your hands open and you're ready to start.

Sometimes it helps to concentrate on something in the room that you are sitting in, like the flame of a candle. This helps focus your attention on one thing.

Repeat in your mind the words, "I am love. I am love. I am love. I am love." You will notice that other thoughts will jump in your mind. Don't fight them. Just allow them to be. When you notice these thoughts continue to say in your mind, "I am love." You may feel sensations in your body; be more conscious of your breath or hearing sounds around you, probably sounds that you were never conscious of before. Once you have done this for a few minutes, bring your attention to your heart. Feel your heart beat. Feel it beat by beat. Stay here for about

CHAPTER 16   How to meditate.

ten seconds, and then bring your awareness to your feet. Feel the aliveness in your feet. You may feel a sensation, warmth, coolness, etc. Then switch to your hands. Feel the energy and focus all of your attention on your hands. You will start to feel your hands; whether that's a tingle, a surge of energy, etc.

Bring your awareness back into your heart and repeat these words: "Love, peace, harmony." Say it softly in your mind. If your thoughts drag you away, that's okay. Just return to these words. Do this for a couple of minutes and then as you wish you can stop.

You've just meditated. The more you do this the better you will become. You will notice that your thoughts will become calmer and you will be distracted by your thoughts less. You will start to see the benefits of meditation and be drawn to it.

Present moment conductors

Have you ever gone for a walk out among nature and listened to the birds chirping, listened to the free flowing water in the river, and really been aware of the sights and sounds around you? You're probably drawn to this type of relaxation. It's a way to calm the mind and rejuvenate your inner being. Or maybe you're an animal lover and you know that being next to your pet makes you feel more alive, re-energizes you, and puts you at peace. Or maybe it just takes being in the presence of a baby. You gaze down at a baby to see her just breathe silently as she sleeps, which deepens your appreciation for the miracle of life.

And for some reason you feel calmer, you feel more relaxed, and you feel more connected with life as a whole.

I call these *present moment conductors*. It's a way of using what's around you to help you concentrate on exactly what's going on right here and now. Some people use exercise as this medium. Intense aerobic and anaerobic exercise can put people in the "zone" or "flow." In psychology, the "flow" is a mental state in which a person who is performing the exercise is fully immersed in a feeling of energized focus, fully aware, and in full enjoyment of whatever they are doing. In other words, "flow" is complete absorption of whatever the person is doing. Other people play sports. Concentrating on exactly what is going on in the present moment, especially in fast pace sports, such as hockey, is vital in playing these sports. If you are playing goalie in a hockey game and have a puck flying to between your eyes at one hundred miles per hour, you are not going to be thinking about the bill you owe that's three months overdue. Sports have a way to bring you out of your mind and absorb you into the present.

Find your own present moment conductor. Maybe you like to play a musical instrument, sing, or maybe you're into bird watching or taking photographs. Maybe you like to knit, build things, or maybe you have a talent that when practicing puts you into this zone.

We all have something that naturally makes us feel good. What a lot of people do not realize is that when they are doing the thing that makes them feel good, they are most likely absorbing themselves completely in the moment. They are resting their minds, giving all their attention to exactly what they are doing, and in effect, their minds are resting. And when their minds are resting, they do not have the ability to be thinking negative thoughts.

Resting your mind is one of the most beneficial things you can do for your health.

Chapter 17

The law of giving.

Whatever you're lacking in life, give it away and see what happens. I realize this seems like it doesn't make sense. And in its structure it sounds paradoxical. But it isn't when you break it down and look at it for what it means.

So many people are lacking love from their families, their spouse, their children, and friends. The human tendency is to complain, ridicule, and point fingers at the person that is not showing their appreciation for you. This is only going to irritate the person that you are lacking love from.

Do you think complaining to your husband that he never cuts the grass will make him want to cut it more? Simply put, this will not make him want to cut the grass. But what happens when you compliment him when he actually does cut the grass? Deep inside he wants to do it that much more the next time because he appreciates your sense of gratitude and this makes him feel good.

If you're lacking love, give it away. Like energy attracts like energy. The receiver of your love will actually change their mood, their brain chemistry will change, and their willingness to provide you with what you're lacking will increase.

Imagine getting into a heated argument with your partner. You both exit each other's presence and slam the door behind you. Well over an hour into being alone, your mind is racing; your thoughts are vengeful. You are just waiting for the opportunity to bring up the past to try to put him/her in their place. Then all of a sudden you hear the bedroom door open and you know she's coming in for another round of arguing. You're ready, you're fierce, and your ego is ready to pounce on every opportunity to make her look bad and make you look good. She walks over, bends down, and kisses you on the forehead and whispers, "I know we both said some hurtful things. I just want to let you know that I love you." She walks out of the room and your ego shrinks. You don't feel the urge to pounce on her anymore. It's like something just swept your ego off its feet.

In order to get what you want, you have to send out the same energy. Period.

You are creating the energy you get back from people. It is absolutely no coincidence that people full of stress will attract more people full of stress. It is absolutely no coincidence that people suffering from agony caused by craving bigger and better superficial things will inevitably attract people of the same nature. It is absolutely no coincidence that people on the path to spirituality will attract others on the same path.

I receive thousands of emails every month, and in so many of the emails the person says how amazed they are that, after implementing what I have taught them, amazing people and situations are just happening to appear in their lives, out of nowhere. They believe it is a coincidence but the reality is that it is absolutely no coincidence at all. The people who are attracted to us are the people that are most like us. Kind people attract kind people. Pessimists attract pessimists. Optimists attract optimists. In order to attract certain people in our lives, we have to be exactly like what we are trying to attract.

We are the creators of exactly what we are putting out. Always. Whatever you lack, give it away, and see what happens.

Chapter 18

Why do we crave?

A while back, I was driving home from a meeting. I decided to turn on the radio for a change, as I typically listen to audio books on my MP3 player. The song that happened to be on the radio was called, "One," by Creed. This has been one of my very favorite songs for years. In my mind I said, "Oh great, I love this song." So of course, I kept it on that station and turned up the volume. I listened to the entire song and was thankful for the timing of turning on the radio station to hear the song. As I listened, I didn't want the song to end.

About three minutes later, the song ended and something really weird hit me. I realized that this song has been on my MP3 player all along, day after day, and I never once (at least in the last year) turned it on. I didn't forget the song was on there. I knew it was there along with most of Creed's other songs. So I asked myself why I chose never to listen to one of my favorite songs when I had the ability to switch it on any time I pleased.

Then the answer hit me. I didn't choose to turn it on because I had so many other options to pick from, newer and fresher music, literally hundreds of songs on demand, from top-40 songs to country and old rock.

It's funny how in life we cherish the things we have until we get bigger and better things. Then the things we originally valued don't hold their value anymore. It's like the first "old-beater" car that a college student saves to buy and is absolutely ecstatic that it takes him from point A to point B. But what happens to that car once that student graduates, gets a job, and has enough money to buy a brand new car? The car that he once valued so much doesn't hold its value any longer.

Why? Because he has a bigger and better "thing." And that bigger and better thing now holds the value that the "old-beater" once did. But the crazy thing is this: give it a few years and that brand new car will not hold the value and importance in his mind anymore. The "bigger and better" car that he is now saving for will hold that value.

We see this every day with every "thing." It's human tendency to crave "bigger and better." But once we achieve it, we crave it all over again. We are in a continual state of craving "better." We believe all the physical things we buy will ultimately bring happiness, but unfortunately, that illusion of happiness only lingers with us for a set period of time; typically, until the "newness" wears off.

In fact, studies suggest that lottery winners were no happier years down the road than before they won the lottery.

Why didn't I ever choose to listen to the song "One" on my MP3 player? Because I had bigger and better to listen to, anytime I wanted. So that song didn't hold the value it did on the radio, because on the radio, I simply can't switch the frequency to magically turn on that particular song.

Money, things, and events will never create real, legitimate happiness within us. Happiness is a state of being that comes from the inside. When we learn to "let go" and not become attached to physical things, we can find happiness in the present moment. When we learn to live in the present (not thinking about the past or future), we can learn to appreciate the small things in life that typically go "unnoticed."

Chapter 19

We all have a little darkness in us.

All humans throughout different parts of their lives have a burning desire to see, feel, or experience "negative" situations. But most people would never admit they wanted to see someone suffer, see crime take place, or see someone in pain.

- Have you ever watched a hockey game and wanted to see two people on the ice fight?

- Did you ever feel envy towards someone who just won the lottery?

- Do you feel jealousy towards your boyfriend or girlfriend when they get to close to the opposite sex?

- Do you just feel like punching a particular someone sometimes?

- How about feeling so happy to be able to gossip about someone you dislike because he/she is going through a hard time?

- How about feeling excitement or a "rush" when you witness a car accident and feel a little disappointed when you "almost" saw one?

- How about feeling the deep urge to beat or even kill someone who has harmed your children physically, emotionally, or sexually?

We all have a dark side to us. Some experts call it our "shadow." The problem is that most of us try to suppress this shadow. We try to deny that it even exists. But what happens over years and years of trying to suppress something? If we bottle up these feelings of hatred, anger, jealousy, and envy, it will eventually creep up on us and explode. These "explosions" usually occur as a fit of rage, anger, jealousy, and even anxiety or depression.

It's not healthy to hide these feelings. It's not healthy to pretend we are all good, all loving, and all peaceful because we are not. No one is. And the people who appear to be nothing but love, peace, and harmony most certainly have dark sides. It's what it means to be human.

We have to learn how to embrace the evil (or whatever you want to call it) side of us. Learn how to use it to our advantage. Instead of bottling up our "true" emotions, we should acknowledge that they exist, allow the feeling to pass, and then move on with our lives. But if we continue to bottle up these negative emotions, they will eventually get the best of us.

Be thankful for all your emotions, both good and bad. They are there for a reason. They help us grow and evolve as people.

It's never a good idea to bottle up what our true nature is. Rest assured our minds/brains are too smart and will always express itself one way or another.

In order to feel love, peace, and harmony, we can't ignore our other emotions. It's impossible to monitor your thousands of thoughts every single day. A very easy way to explore what thoughts you are thinking is to ask yourself what you are feeling. Your emotions are always a reflection of what you are thinking. If you are feeling sad, you are thinking negative thoughts. If you are feeling good, you are thinking positive thoughts.

Let's try to end with love but work with what we have.

Monster downstairs

Let's pretend . . .

There is a monster, a very scary, demonic looking creature that lives in your basement. He's so scary and violent that you actually have him locked down there. You never turn on the lights for him and you feel so ashamed and embarrassed that he lives in your basement. You feed him by throwing scraps down the stairs, not because you want to, but because he screams so loudly until he is fed that you would never be able to sleep or even do any work. Sometimes the food reaches him and sometimes it doesn't, as he can barely reach the stairs, because he's tied up securely with a chain around his neck that is bolted onto a large cement poll used to support the ceiling. On days when the sun is shining at the perfect angle through your porch door, you can see his ugly face peeking through the darkness awaiting his meal.

CHAPTER 19 We all have a little darkness in us.

You hate him, and try your best to go on about your day not revealing to anyone that he lives with you. How could you possibly release your secret that this evil creature lives under your roof? Sometimes when you leave town for a few days and forget to feed him, he gets so mad at you, so vicious that he destroys everything in his path, tears holes in the walls, and tears his neck to pieces by trying to break free from the chain.

But something happened over the years. As you continued to curse him, feed him, and ignore his constant requests to allow him to come upstairs, he decided to take you on for all that you were worth. Over the years, he grew into this huge beast. You didn't realize this as you never once went down to see him. One day when you were out of the house, he actually got the strength to break out of the restraints, climb up the stairs, and tear your whole house to pieces. Room for room he destroyed everything. When you arrived home, you opened the door to see him in your living room, down on his four legs, saliva dripping from his mouth, growling, just waiting to attack you. Before you got a chance to open the door to escape, he pounced on you ripping your cloths to shreds. He bit and scratched you and it seemed as though the more you bled the more vicious he became. There was no one around to hear your screams and he didn't seem to care that he was killing you. You were losing so much blood that you lost all energy to fight back. And just when it seemed that all hope was lost and you were about to die, he got off you, lowered his head, and walked downstairs into the basement.

You couldn't believe it. You were so thankful that he let you live. As you rushed to the hospital, you couldn't help but wonder not only why he didn't kill you, but also why after the attack he walked himself downstairs. It was as if he was trying to say, "Don't lock me up. Don't mistreat me. Don't ignore me, and don't hate me. I am a part of your life whether or not you like me. Get used to living with me. And if you don't treat me with respect, I will attack when you least expect it."

Obviously, you don't have a monster that lives in your basement. But the fact of the matter is, we all have monsters that live within us. Call it hate, jealously, anger, rage, or any other negative emotion we dislike. For the most part, we try to hide these feelings. We trap them inside just like you trapped the monster in your basement. But over the years these emotions build, they get stronger just like the monster. And then, suddenly, something in life triggers them and they all go off simultaneously with a vicious attack that we can't control. Sometimes this attack could be a fit of rage, anger, hatred, or even anxiety or depression.

If we continue to bottle up these "so called" negative emotions, they will ultimately get the best of us in some way or another. Everyone has feelings of hatred, anger, jealousy, and resentment. These feelings are completely normal and nothing to be embarrassed or ashamed over. This is what it means to be human.

We have to learn to allow these feelings to express themselves in a "productive" way before they grow to the point where we can't control them.

Rest assured our bodies and brains are too intelligent to

allow us to bottle our true emotions up inside of us. They will always show themselves when we least expect them.

Allow the monster to breathe. Acknowledge it. Give thanks for it. It lives in us for a reason—to help us grow, learn, and appreciate things we didn't appreciate before.

The more we acknowledge the negative emotions; we begin to see that these emotions are being created by the ego. By using the methods described in this book, you can tame the ego, step by step to the point where these negative emotions are not a predominant part of your life and then you can start to live a life void of the grips of the ego. This is one of the most liberating feelings you can experience here on earth.

Chapter 20

Does everything happen for a reason?

We have all heard the phrase, "Everything happens for a reason." You have probably said it to comfort a friend who is going through a breakup or to try to make your brother or sister who has been laid off from a job feel better. Do you actually believe this phrase or are you just saying it to help someone through a difficult time?

When you look deeply into the statement and try to understand what it truly means, something special begins to show itself. Is there any truth to the statement, "Everything happens for a reason," and if so, what is the reason and why is it happening?

I believe every single event that happens in the course of my life, your life, and in fact, every event that has ever unfolded throughout the beginning of time has a purpose. The purpose, especially during a difficult incident such as a death in the family is very hard to understand and accept, because our emotions are interfering with our level of rationale.

CHAPTER 20 **Does everything happen for a reason?**

What is the secret to this statement?

You will notice that the people who believe everything happens for a reason tend to be optimistic people. This is because of their perception of life. When something, so called "negative" happens in the life of an optimistic person, they automatically believe it is happening for the greater good. This belief automatically trains their eyes to notice the opportunities that arise out of the "negative" situation, which if acted upon, will better their lives somehow. So, in other words, their belief that everything happens for a reason actually helps them notice that reason.

For instance, if an optimistic person were to lose their job, they would look at the brighter side of the situation, realizing this is a great opportunity, a chance to start the business they always dreamt of.

A pessimist, on the other hand, would look at the difficult situation as just that, a difficult situation. They have hard wired their brains to not look at what's beyond the corner or what could await them. Therefore, everything does not happen for a reason, for them. And because they truly believe this, their eyes are not going to notice all the opportunities that could have turned that difficult situation into something special.

We create the "reason" by our outlook, perspective, and attitude. When you start to change your thinking about your reality and start to realize that everything truly does happen for a reason, then your world becomes something really amazing.

Chapter 21

Imagine not being from this earth.

Let's imagine that you were another life form from another distant planet. You didn't actually have a body; you were a floating essence of consciousness not able to see with eyes, taste with a tongue, smell with a nose, touch with fingers, or hear with ears. You had no idea what it was like to live in a human body. But even though you don't know what it's like to be human, you are aware of what the human race is doing not only to destroy the planet but also what they are doing on a daily basis to destroy themselves. You see their baffling behaviors and it confuses you as to why they do what they do. You wish you had the opportunity to walk a day in their shoes and experience the world of a human being.

Then you are given a chance for your soul/spirit to enter into a physical body. You suddenly are sucked down to earth to join other fellow human beings.

Your very first experience as a human being is when you woke up in bed. You open your eyes and your initial response is how your back feels pressed against a nice, warm, comfortable

CHAPTER 21   Imagine not being from this earth.

bed. You are so grateful that you have the sense of feeling. Before opening your eyes, you hear the clock ticking and the birds singing. You then feel the sun beaming down on your eyelids. It feels so peaceful and is just enough brightness to stimulate you enough to open your eyes. You open your eyes to feel the warmth of the sun. This is something you have never experienced before and you are so thankful for the opportunity to see it. Then you feel and hear your belly make weird noises. You understand this is hunger. You stand up, walk towards the kitchen, and feel so thankful that you are able to experience the feeling of walking, using two feet, two legs, and balance to get to where you're headed. You know that what you eat fuels the body. You feel so blessed and thankful that you now have a body to enjoy and experience, and you know that you are going to fuel it with the best food you can possibly find. You know what's good and you know what's bad.

You walk to the local supermarket and buy the best organic, fresh food. You eat it and it fuels you with genuine energy the body needs in order to thrive. You go for a walk down a busy street and you take everything in, the clean air, the people talking, jogging, and walking their dogs. In fact, every dog you see, you stop to ask the owner if you can pet the animal. The owner always smiles and invites you to do so. You take the opportunity every time as you know that appreciating all life forms calms the mind and releases chemicals that help boost your immune system and help you feel great.

After walking for so long, you decide to run, as you want to use your body the way it's supposed to be used. You sweat, you feel your muscles ache, your heart races, and you breathe rapid and fast. It's great to feel your body change as you're exercising it the way it's meant to be exercised. During this process, your brain releases endorphins and once again, you feel fantastic!

Throughout the day, you are drinking lots of water. You know this keeps the body in great health and helps move any toxins out of you, maintains the balance of your bodily floods, hydrates you, gives you energy, boosts your immune system, and helps you feel better about yourself.

You smile at the people you see because you know that your smile, even for a second, helps make them feel better about themselves and their day. You offer to help an old lady cross the street and your reward that you anticipate is not money, recognition, or praise. Your reward is that you know you made that lady's day a little easier with your gesture of kindness.

You find a river and sit down next to it. You gaze at the ducks and other wildlife that occupies the water and the air. Each and every flap of the bird's wings you are aware of and you notice how peaceful they are flowing through the air. Their actions, sounds, and gentleness stills you, quiets you, and you feel so connected to everything around you.

You sit quietly and relax your mind, as you know the mind is not meant to be thinking all day. You sit still, close your eyes, and become aware of all the sounds around you. You intensely listen to the birds sing; flap their wings, and the ducks quacking. You hear the footsteps of the people running behind you, the conversations happening within your distance, and the waves of the stream. You are aware of everything around you. You are

CHAPTER 21   Imagine not being from this earth.

not thinking about yesterday and you are not thinking about tomorrow. You are still. You are present. You know when the mind is still and not thinking, you are boosting your immune system and releasing all the chemicals into your bloodstream that contribute to health and well-being. After five minutes of meditation, you open your eyes and feel so rejuvenated.

As you are walking back to your home, you feel the grass beneath your feet; you breathe deeply into your diaphragm, and feel the cool breeze against your skin. You spend the remainder of the day giving gratitude for the experiences you've had, the food you have used to fuel your body, and for the sun to nourish your body and soul.

As you lay down to fall asleep, you once again feel the bed with every part of your body that is touching it. You gaze up at the moon and note all the differences you feel and see from when you initially looked at the sun. You feel calm, happy, and so gracious that you were able to walk a day in the life of a human being.

The next morning you wake up and you want to try an experiment. Now that you know what it's like to walk in the shoes of a human being for one day, you want to see how and why others live the particular way they do. So you scope out someone who seems to live quite differently than the way you lived your first day as a human being. You follow this person; you study this person, and you try to understand why they continue to abuse their body the way they do.

You notice the very first thing Bob does when he arises is drink coffee because he does not have enough energy to go about his morning without this stimulant. You ask yourself why he uses such a stimulant when he has everything in him and around him to develop the needed energy. He doesn't eat breakfast and goes straight to work. You notice he seems to complain about his work and you feel sorry that he has to be at a place he dreads forty hours a week. Every single time he complains about his work, you can see his energy level drops. You also know that every time he complains, he reminds himself of the discomfort that he does not want to live in, which then, of course, releases the chemicals into the body that weakens his immune system, creating stress and anxiety. It seems as though nothing goes his way. But at the same time you notice he does not notice or give thanks to the things that he can be grateful for. Because he concentrates on the things he does not like, he seems to hate life more and more with each complaining breath he takes. His relationships at work are not friendly and in fact, he downright hates some of the people he deals with at the facility where he works.

He arrives home later that evening and the first thing he craves is alcohol. He craves this because he wants to turn off his mind. He wants to forget about all the agonizing things that he thinks about on a regular basis. So, he sits back, starts to drink, and finally feels better. It takes the edge off. But what he does not realize is that this relaxation is only temporary. You want to scream at him and tell him that this is not the right thing to do. You want to tell him that the agony can be taken away but it can't be taken away by drinking a toxin. But you stand back and watch what he does, step for step. As he continues to drink, he watches television and starts to laugh. He seems happy. He seems calm. And he believes in the illusion that a toxic substance can make him happy.

CHAPTER 21   Imagine not being from this earth.

He goes to sleep half "buzzed" and wakes up to another dreaded day.

You meditate on what has happened; how both your days could be so dramatically different. You meditate on how lives can be so different and you realize that everything related back to his thoughts about life. You realize that he created his own hell on earth. You realized his constant pessimistic attitude, neglect to appreciate the good things in his life, and his willingness to numb his mind with alcohol were all attracting more and more things that he will dread.

You are sucked back up to your planet, sit in silence, and think, "If I ever get the experience to live a full life on earth, I will treat my mind and body as the greatest gift I could ever receive."

Chapter 22

It's the year 3000.

In a meditation, I imagined it was the year 3000, much different than today, 2014. Here were my thoughts . . .

I can't believe that back in the twenty-first century people were actually locked behind bars for the mistakes they made, physically confined into areas no bigger than bedrooms, sometimes for the duration of their entire life. It seems as though the authority figures just didn't realize that everyone makes mistakes but no one should have the ability to subject an individual to punishment, torture, and a life full of resentment, hatred, and ridicule.

Thank God, I live in a world today where people's mistakes are regarded as mistakes, where our very first action towards wrongdoers is help, rehabilitation, and understanding as opposed to punishment, hatred, and violence. Although it's important to recognize wrong actions made by people, it's equally important to recognize they need love, not punishment. Why couldn't these people understand that you can't fight fire with fire and produce anything other than fire? It seems as though most people back then didn't realize that mistakes and acts of perceived evil were performed because of the immense amount of influential circumstances the perceived "wrongdoer" was exposed to during his/her life.

Thank God, I live in a world where rehabilitation and authentic love is more powerful than the urge to punish.

It seems as though money and fame back then were more important than happiness, peace, and kindness. Even in the education systems, youth weren't taught how to rest their minds but for the most part taught to over-activate their minds with complex math formulas, chemistry equations, and physics problems. I guess they didn't realize resting your mind as opposed to over-activating it is one of the key elements of peace and fulfillment. It just seems to me that their type of education was mostly about being successful in the work place as opposed to learning the true nature of happiness, health, and well-being.

Thank God, I live in a world where the most important education is concerned with happiness, peace, and purpose as opposed to business, wealth, and fortune.

It's so disturbing that people allowed their own understandings and perceptions to interfere with their happiness. They allowed their belief in the afterlife, Gods, and religion to actually justify hatred, crime, and even war. It seems that their level of understanding was so primitive. They actually allowed their differences in beliefs to affect the way they perceive and treat others.

Thank God, I live in a world where accepting other's beliefs is second nature and judgment of differences is scarce.

But of all the differences that saddened me, the one that sticks out in my mind the most is how people in the twenty-first century actually allowed ethnicity, color, and social status to define who they were. It seemed as though they believed that where a person was from, how wealthy they were, or what color their skin was allowed them to pinpoint how important they were. It seemed as though they didn't realize we are all the same, all connected, all one.

Thank God, the differences that existed in the twenty-first century don't exist today.

Chapter 23

What does it mean to be awakened?

Being awakened means that you see reality the way it truly is. It means that you wake up from your sleep or your everyday life, and start to live in a completely different perspective, in a different light.

You know you're starting to awaken when . . .

- You don't blame situations for the stress or anxiety that you are experiencing.

- You realize that it is your thoughts that create stress and anxiety.

- You are aware that a large majority of the time most people are living completely unconsciously, acting in complete accordance to their subconscious beliefs that were implanted in them year after year from what they were exposed to.

- When you know that pharmaceutical drugs never treat the cause of the illness, but only mask the symptom.

- When you realize that one of the most important things you can do to attract positive people and positive situations into your life is to project love, peace, and kindness. Like energy always attracts like energy.

- When you realize that judgment is always a reflection of the person doing the judging.

- When you realize that whatever energy you emotionally recognize in someone else is within you.

- When you realize you feel love and compassion towards criminals as opposed to hate and vengeance.

- When you realize you attract whatever you think about.

- When you realize one of the best things you can do to help someone in need is to visualize them in perfect health and harmony.

- When you realize that you are perfect, whole, and beautiful, no matter how much you weigh, how you look, or how old you are.

- When you realize that giving gratitude for the things you have in your life actually attracts more things to be thankful for.

- When you realize you are the creator of your everything.

Chapter 24

Going against the grain.

The Transition Period

Once incorporating the techniques described in this book a lot of people go through what I refer to as, "The transition period." For the first few days, weeks or even months, after applying these techniques, people feel energized, motivated, and overall healthier. But sometimes the transition period kicks in and the ego tries to creep back into the mind. This is the ego's final attack. Because of the healthier lifestyle that the person is now living the person's mind (ego) is not going to enjoy the change.

I hear a lot of people tell me that they are bored on the weekends because they were used to going out to clubs. I hear others tell me that they miss their friends that they no longer associate with. Other types of discomfort may creep up on you. It's important to realize that this is the ego's last swipe at you, trying to get you to retreat and fall into your old lifestyle. Rest assured that once you get through this transition period life becomes easier and the ego then retreats. You no longer miss your old friends as much because you made new positive friends. You no longer are bored on the weekends because you have found new healthy activities to occupy your time with. So many people fall into the ego's last attempt to pull them back into the grips of negativity. If they would have just stuck it out a little while longer they would have defeated the ego and built a new "normal." Once this new normal is built the ego is no longer possessing the mind and life becomes bliss.

You are probably reading this chapter thinking, "Wow, this is so much that I have to do to get rid of my stress, anxiety, and depression." And on some level, yes, you are correct. But what you have to realize is that these techniques are not really techniques, they are the way that we are meant to live as a human. We have been so warped to believe in certain things, act in certain ways, consume poisons that are destroying our bodies. Because mostly everyone else lives this way, we thought it was the right way to live. But the truth is that it is not. Just because everyone else is living a particular way that does not mean you should live that way too.

When I was living a life crippled with anxiety, I had no idea what was causing it. I had no idea why I lost all my gumption to do the things that previously brought me joy. I had no idea why my life had turned into a life of torment, hatred, and confusion. But it was those experiences, that life of torment, that brought me to not only my level of appreciation that I now experience every single day of my life, but it also pushed me to understand why anxiety exists. It exists to send us a warning signal that we, not necessarily situations, have to change. We are the cause of why we are experiencing anxiety and stress. We are the cause of everything that we experience.

CHAPTER 24   **Going against the grain.**

I have presented for tens of thousands of people all over the world and the message has helped so many. But the message is only a message. Without application, the message becomes useless. I have many people that come to many of my presentations, so I get to see their familiar faces, sometimes, several times a year. They come up to me after the presentation, thank me, and tell me how much my techniques have been helping them. Some of them say that by complaining, judging, and gossiping less, and meditating more it has eliminated so much of their stress and anxiety. But then they tell me that it's not completely gone. So I ask them about the other techniques that I teach and if they are using them. So many of them say, "Well, I am doing so many of your techniques but I still drink." It is no surprise their anxiety still exists if they continue to drink alcohol. Alcohol numbs the mind and when the mind is artificially being numbed, it is robbing nature's ability to create resilience. This will inevitably lead to a lack of coping skills, which will then lead to stress and anxiety.

I see so many people struggling, day by day. I have received tens of thousands of emails from all over the world. These people are desperately reaching out for help and advice. They are lost, completely lost. They feel hopeless. They believe that they are a victim of the life situation and this will be their reality forever. And the sad reality is that if they believe it to be true, then it will be true. After presenting to thousands of people all over, I have heard thousands of stories. Some of the stories are so difficult to hear because I was once where these people are.

So many times, people come up to me after my presentations and tell me that the presentation has given them a whole new perspective on life and they now have hope again. When I hear this, it motivates me to continue to share my message to as many people as I possibly can. What most people do not know about me is that, before I wrote my first book, *The Power of the Mind: How I Beat OCD*, I made a promise to myself to never, ever release this secret part of my life. I was embarrassed. I was ashamed. And I was so scared of what other people would think about me. But after I started to recover and started to love life again, my conscience would kick in morning after morning and tell me that sharing my story could help a lot of people. Still, the fear of releasing my story would take over my mind and I would decide not to share it with anyone. Day after day, my conscience would talk to me and try to convince me that sharing my story was the right thing to do. I finally realized that if the young girl in the magazine (who I talked about in Chapter 2), who shared her story of growing up with Obsessive Compulsive Disorder, did not have the courage to share her story with the world, I have no idea if I would even be alive today. This revelation really affected me and I finally developed the courage to speak out and share what I promised I would never share with the world.

For several years before sharing my story, I was speaking professionally on the strength of thoughts and the power of the mind, but I had never told my story to anyone. Finally, after building up the courage, I talked about my story for the very first time at a local presentation I was giving on the strength of human thoughts. What I shared that night was so brief I thought it would not have an effect on the audience that I was speaking to. If my memory serves me correctly, the only thing I said was something along the lines of, "I have used what I have just taught you over the last two hours to help me overcome mental health issues that I was facing years ago." I then talked a little more about the mind and thanked the audience for coming out to the presentation.

I later went home and received email after email from my audience members asking what kind of mental health issue I had. And there was story after story about what they were going through or their loved ones were going through. The emails continued to come in one after the other asking how I could help them get through their anxiety and depression. I then realized how important my story was to the world. I knew that I went through what I went through to help others dealing with something similar. I knew that there was a greater purpose to my life than what I previously understood. Not all of my experiences leading me up until that exact moment were happening to me; they were happening for me.

Sharing my story with the world was one of the best decisions I have ever made. Because of this, I have met so many amazing people and heard so many amazing stories of recovery. Although I may not be able to return every single email, people have no idea how much their emails mean to me. Each and every one encourages me. I am so blessed to have the opportunity to do what I do. And looking back at my struggle, I now thank God for every situation I have been through that has lead me to this point.

We have to open our eyes and realize how we are meant to live and where stress and anxiety truly come from. When we stop believing in the lies of society and start looking at the facts, we realize that we can take complete ownership of our lives and shape the life we want to. We realize that we can completely get rid of unneeded stress, anxiety, and depression. We can live a life of peace, passion, enthusiasm, love, and even more important, want to share this with not only our loved ones but with the world.

If I could tell one message to this world, it would be that our thoughts create us. Our thoughts determine everything that we are attracted to. Our thoughts are the creation of our everything. Knowing this one truth has the potential to completely transform someone's life. Knowing this truth has the potential to save lives. Knowing this truth has the potential to save humanity and transform us into a loving, peaceful world.

I challenge you to take ownership over your life. I challenge you to start embracing life and to start by giving and feeling appreciation to what you currently have in your life. I challenge you to start using the techniques described in this book. I challenge you to change your perception of why you are suffering. I challenge you to stop being a victim of your circumstances. And I challenge you to build yourself into exactly who you are meant to be.

When you can walk in peace, love, and harmony in the midst of a chaotic world, you are awakened.

You create your everything.

God bless.

Other books by the author

At the age of twelve, he developed a severe case of anxiety and an overwhelming need to exert control over it. Doctors said it was one of the worst cases of OCD they had ever seen. Furthermore, they told him it was incurable, that the incessant counting, tapping, opening and closing of doors—and myriad other repetitive behaviours—would stay with him for the rest of his life.

They were wrong.

Often a crippling mental disorder, OCD is the fourth most commonly diagnosed mental illness. This is the incredible true story of one man's triumph over it.

Jeremy Bennett Bio

Jeremy Bennett is an international mental health advocate, speaker, television producer/host, and travels the world educating his audiences on the astonishing power of human thoughts in relation to health and wellness. He is known as having one of the most unique presentations on the mind. His work continues to be endorsed and praised by some of the most respected doctors worldwide.

For more information on Jeremy or to book him to speak at an event please visit

www.jeremybennett.ca

Also "Like" Jeremy on **Facebook**:

www.facebook.com/jeremybennettfanpage

and follow him on **Twitter**:

@Jeremy_Bennett

CPSIA information can be obtained at www.ICGtesting.com
Printed in the USA
BVOW06s1408150716

455392BV00013B/193/P